Praise for *The Energy of Abundance*

"From the moment I started to read *The Energy of Abundance* I felt a wave of gratitude that this break-through-it book has finally been written. Phyllis King masterfully and lovingly brings to light powerful new ways of understanding how energy works in our lives. She gives you easy-to-apply tools to awaken new possibilities and achieve fulfillment of your dreams in every area of your life. A must read for anyone seeking to change their life for the better."

—Sheri Meyers, Psy.D. Marriage and Family Therapist, best-selling author of "Chatting or Cheating"

THE
Energy
OF
Abundance

PRACTICAL ADVICE AND
SPIRITUAL WISDOM TO ACHIEVE
ANYTHING YOU WANT IN LIFE

Phyllis King

The Career Press, Inc.
Wayne, NJ

THE ENERGY OF ABUNDANCE
TYPESET BY KRISTIN GOBLE
Cover design by Dutton and Sherman Design
Printed in the U.S.A.

To order this title, please call toll-free 1-800-CAREER-1 (NJ and Canada: 201-848-0310) to order using VISA or MasterCard, or for further information on books from Career Press.

The Career Press, Inc.
www.careerpress.com
www.newpagebooks.com

Library of Congress Cataloging-in-Publication Data
King, Phyllis.
    The energy of abundance : practical advice and spiritual wisdom to achieve anything you want in life / by Phyllis King ; foreword by Dr. Joe Vitale. -- 1
        pages cm
        Summary: "The Energy of Abundance is a fresh, insightful, and often humorous view of life, spirituality, and the creative process. It explains in accessible language the "energy game," and how each of us can play it to invite more happiness, love, and abundance into our lives"-- Provided by publisher.
    Includes bibliographical references and index.
    ISBN 978-1-63265-005-4 (paperback) -- ISBN 978-1-63265-993-4 (ebook) 1. Self-actualization (Psychology) 2. Success. 3. Happiness. 4. Spiritual life. I. Title.

BF637.S4K54844 2015
158--dc23

                                                                    2015002858

This work is dedicated to Maya and Leo, and
all the amazing souls who have invited me into their energy.

ACKNOWLEDGMENTS

It takes a village.

I want to thank Career Press and New Page Books for the opportunity to share the message of the Energy Game.

I thank my dearest friends, Donna Morrish, Jennifer Barton, Sarah Kinghan, Venetia Kinghan, and Walter Zajac for your relentless and unwaivering support and love.

My deepest gratitude to Dr. Joe Vitale, Dannion Brinkley, Vaishali, Nayaswami Asha Praver, John Assaraf, Dr. Sheri Meyers, and Katherine Woodward Thomas for your wisdom and your work. You have lifted me up. I am a better person and able to offer more to the world because of you.

Special thanks to Bill Gladstone and Margot Hutchison of the Waterside Agency for opening the door to greater possibilities for me.

DISCLAIMER

All names and identities have been changed to protect the privacy of those involved, and whose stories inspired the writing of this book.

TABLE OF CONTENTS

FOREWORD

Have you ever gone to a psychic?

I have. Lots. Most of the time they aren't accurate, but they're usually entertaining. Well, forget the side shows at the circus and the tents at a New Age fair. It's time for you to meet the real deal—and she's entertaining *and* accurate. In fact, she's known as "The Common Sense Psychic."

Phyllis King is remarkable. After 15 years of being a professional psychic to tens of thousands of people in 25 countries, she decided to help even more people by writing this book. Not only can she read auras and energy, but she has the street-smart wisdom to help you understand what she sees. In other words, she cuts through the bull to get you past your own stuff. She moves you onto a spiritual realization that abundance is not only your natural birth right, it's been waiting for you all along.

This sparkling book is like having Phyllis at your side. She's a delight. She is sitting with you, having a cup of tea, and talking to you. She carefully, lovingly, and clearly helps you understand key areas of your life, from relationships to life purpose, to karma, marriage, parenting, and more.

As I was reading this book, I felt like another door was opening within my heart. I felt more grounded, more expanded, more loving, more understanding, and more aware. As much as I read, this is quite an accomplishment. It made me feel like the book was alive—an oracle of wisdom. Open it anywhere and let the words speak.

For example, at one point she advises people to discover their life purpose by paying attention to what is showing up in each moment. If there are reoccurring issues, it is a sign pointing to what needs resolving. She says, "All the individual has to do is identify the feeling they have in the moment. Whatever the feeling is, that's what needs to be considered your life purpose for the moment. Clear it and move on."

I also loved the stories. Talking about the Beatles as a way to teach about reincarnation is entertaining and educational. Because I'm a musician as well as an author, this story, and more, kept me reading with fascination and a smile.

This wonderful book is designed to help you in numerous ways, from how to connect to your abundant core and how to release beliefs that don't serve you, to how to attract the prosperity, relationships, and more that you long to achieve.

You are in for a treat. I'm no psychic, but I predict you will love this book. Phyllis King has opened the vault to the secrets of an abundant universe. All you have to do is turn the page....

With Love,
Dr. Joe Vitale
Author of way too many books to list here
A star in the movie *The Secret*
www.MrFire.com

PREFACE

Life is an endless continuum of opportunity. It doesn't matter what family we were born into, or what are our life chances are based upon our history. The universe is waiting for us to embrace abundance that is promised to each of us. It takes courage and determination to receive it. Being in the human experience is not for wimps.

Life is a journey of expansion through self-realization. Through realized self, we inch our way to enlightenment. There is no such thing as a right or wrong answer. There are only answers that free us from self-imposed beliefs in limitation. In this work, it is my intention to give the reader ideas and concepts to help unlock their own insight and information about their unique story. In so doing, it will lead you to your abundant core.

INTRODUCTION

When I began writing books 15 years ago, I did it for myself. I think that is where most people begin their process of contribution. Although I am considered a life management expert, I am always learning and adjusting my point of view based upon new information. Even in this process, with the newest book, I found myself challenged and required to submit to the very processes I ask the reader to undertake. Life is really a continuum. There is no beginning and end, just moments that help us define who we are to ourselves and continue to bring us closer to our truth.

As you begin this journey with me through this book, know there is no end game, just an acceptance of learning to be in the now with peace. Hopefully as you approach new challenges and struggles in your life, you will find encouragement through these pages that help you maintain peace and happiness as your way of being in life.

With love and appreciation,
Phyllis

CHAPTER 1

The Energy Game
(How It Works)

*"Energy cannot be created or destroyed. It can
only be changed from one form to another."*

—ALBERT EINSTEIN

To me, the word *energy* is synonymous with life. This includes tangible matter, intangible matter, emotions, thoughts, and anything the mind can consider or anything we can speak about. I interpret the world as energy moving around in all places at all times. It is my natural state of perception. No one taught me to see life this way. I had a natural skill set of heightened awareness that became apparent at an early age. My experience insisted I seek out and answer questions about why I saw things in a manner others didn't.

The world I live in is fluid and changing all the time on all levels. After decades of observing life through this perception, I came to name our relationship to life the *Energy Game*. Each chapter that follows offers a perspective on a life topic through the eyes of the Energy Game, and how it relates to any of us who want to realize abundance, love, or peace in our lifetime.

I was never a big fan of science growing up. I didn't gravitate toward science naturally. I was a musician raised in a musical family. I enjoyed learning about the earth and animals, and the basics we receive in general education in school. When I began to pursue an understanding of myself, the study and the science of quantum physics became extraordinarily fascinating to me. The theories and study of quantum physics literally validated who I was and am to myself. Somebody, actually a lot of some bodies (Albert Einstein, Niels Bohr, Werner Heisenborg, and Robert Lanza)— suddenly made sense of me in scientific terminology. They explained to me what it is I do and how I relate to life in scientific terms. These people, these scientists, who did not know me, described what I do and what I see. That was and is very exciting to me. It lets me know that me and people like me are simply misunderstood, and that modern culture is on the cusp of gaining the language and the technology to validate how people like me interact with life.

Beyond what it means to me personally as Phyllis King, it's exciting for everyone who can grasp the basic concepts. Quantum physics is a deep and far-reaching science. For purposes of this sharing, I begin with the basic idea that what you think and feel about something alters it. We as observers influence what happens in our own universe by what we perceive to be happening. Please read that again. It is a life-changing idea. It lets us know that we are powerful creative beings living in a fluid universe. We can influence and even master our experience. We are powerful beyond what the mind in the physical body can comprehend as reasonable.

This effect of observation and perspective is something I have been watching and playing with for more than 30 years. The reality of influencing matter, both tangible and intangible, is what gets me amazingly excited about life, about people and our possibilities on the planet. The Energy Game is a simplified method to understand how we can effect change in our lives to live a more abundant, peaceful, and loving existence.

What Does Energy Look Like?

People have always asked me how I am able to "read" energy or see things so clearly. The question is usually "How do you do that?" They really want to know. The manner in which I deliver information is practical and linear in fashion. People expect they should be able to understand it in a linear way. It is a process of observation but also of feeling. When I first began to explain it, I would say "Well, I see patterns," "Sometimes they look like mathematical equations," and "Sometimes they look like schematics." That description took people a certain distance, but didn't quite clear it up for them, in part because it is experiential in nature. You can only go so far with the mind to understand what I do. I allow myself to become aware of the intangible. Many people deny or doubt the existence of the intangible world. You can't understand something you can't be open to.

Once you grasp the marriage between the tangible and intangible, much of the process is practice and getting used to seeing patterns repeat, feeling the textures of situations, and watching how momentums develop. It's more of a process of listening than seeing. I use the word *see*, but it doesn't translate exactly. I actually believe that being a musician helped me hone my intuitive skill set, as playing music is all about listening.

As I continued along in my own personal journey, I encountered a lot of books and ideas on energy. That awareness led me to quantum physics. What is even more fascinating in this discussion is that no one really knows how to define the word *energy*. If you Google the word *energy*, you'll get dozens of definitions. Depending upon your reason for defining energy, each definition will have a value to it. The Dave Watson definition says, "Energy is a property or characteristic (or trait or aspect?) of matter that makes things happen, or, in the case of stored or potential energy, has the 'potential' to make things happen." A Yahoo dictionary search reveals "Capacity for work or vigorous activity; vitality or intensity of expression."

Essentially no one can really say what energy is or isn't. What we do is describe what energy does and how it behaves. For me this word *energy* describes everything I have ever looked at, seen, or experienced as a person with heightened awareness. If we pay attention we can see, feel, and watch energy create our life experiences.

Energy Explained

Everything is energy. Every thought, everything tangible and intangible, is energy. This includes feelings, ideas, and physical objects. Beyond this, tangible and intangible things can have their own consciousness. This idea of consciousness is important to grasp. A consciousness itself is what creates energy. Energy produces the tangible outcomes we experience. There is a natural sequence.

What we put into consciousness will determine the content of our outcomes in life. When I am working with people, it is to help them cultivate and nurture the consciousness they are working inside of at a particular point in time. For instance, for someone with money troubles, I have to help them dis-identify with their scarcity consciousness. It almost always goes back to "Am I worthy? Do I deserve?" There are layers upon layers of conditioning people do to themselves to create a scarcity reality. My work often is one of peeling back layers of conditioning.

This is a whole-being approach, not a compartmentalized approach toward abundance. Our money is not in one place, our health in another, and our relationships in another. The thread of scarcity will run through every area of our being. It shows up in conversation and language, in behavior and in emotional integrity.

I know that when the consciousness is abundant, the tangible matter or experience will feel abundant. We have to take the ego out of it. A person may have a goal to make one million dollars or to cultivate a relationship. Either can be achieved strategically, which is another discussion. If we cultivate a consciousness of abundance, it takes the effort out of the process. Effort does not equate with working hard. It means emotionally effortless. That in our process, we are not in fear. We are not trying to control everything. We are not worrying about our creative process or our outcomes. Rather we are in a state of trust married to clear intention, fueled by hard work or shaping energy. The outcome we want resonates at a certain frequency and requires a certain level of energy. We have to generate enough energy to meet the requirements of the outcome. It's an exchange.

If we want to allow abundance to drive our experience, we have to have a way to get in the flow of divine wisdom. That is an open position of listening and responding to the inner voice, while behaving in life in an open position. If we bathe in frequencies of effort, we push energy in a way that is not in our best interest. It will only take us so far. We have to discover ways around the maze of conditioning in our being to allow divine abundance to flow in our lives. This is the dance most people are learning to master. It takes courage and determination. It is doable.

Our ability to "go with the flow" of life, rather than resist it or get in the way of it, is half the battle of creating the life of our dreams. For instance, energetically, effort is a mid-level frequency. On the spectrum of low- to high-vibration frequencies, high and spacious frequencies have the most potential for benevolent outcomes. Mid-level frequencies bring us to mid-level outcomes. It is when we allow high frequencies to govern our consciousness that we watch miracles and synchronicities occur all around us.

Cassandra's story

The story that follows illustrates how consciousness creates our life. In Cassandra's story, there are multiple layers, as there are in all of our lives. The first aspect of her story reinforces that life is always urging us to heal. Life is inherently benevolent and loving toward us. In our experiences, we attract what we need to learn and heal. Life is always a mirror. What we put into consciousness energetically determines the exchange that comes to us.

Whether we are consciously aware or not, for all of us our ultimate goal is spiritual enlightenment. No matter where we fall on the continuum, we are on our way there. Our consciousness will always create experiences that lead us to areas we need to heal in order to elevate ourselves into a higher state of being. When we can slow down enough to watch our process and listen, we will heal of our own accord. From healing we grow, and from growth we receive.

I had a client named Cassandra, who was a successful property manager of an enormous living community. She was experiencing difficulty with one of her primary contractors on the property. She described their interaction as "He's slacking off," "He is behaving in an adversarial manner toward me," and "He blows up at anything I say." I was able to see, as you the reader can see, that there is a pattern in this interaction. My first comment was "So we have a classic power struggle here." Cassandra, although very capable and experienced, was extremely stressed out by this situation. She was thrown off of her game. Her approach to solutions was entirely from the perspective of "getting him in line" or having to "confront" him or potentially "fire" him.

Cassandra was working from a consciousness that said "I have to control everything. If I don't control everything the outcome will be awful." That consciousness excludes divine collaboration. It's like a hand squeezed tightly. There is no room for any energy to come in. My job was to help Cassandra see how her consciousness was based in control and scarcity. As we moved into the discussion, many layers of contracted frequencies became apparent in her story.

The first step I took with Cassandra was to take the attention off of the contractor and turn her focus to her own reactions and perceptions about what was happening. Whenever any of us are highly emotional in our reactions, meaning we have lost our balance, 99 times out of 100, the emotion is tied to past-time trauma. The event in the present moment has triggered a reservoir of unresolved pain. That results in the potency of the reaction.

Cassandra experienced abuse on many levels throughout her life. She often had adult authority figures punish her for being a truth-teller or being smart. If she spoke up about injustice or punitive treatment she paid dearly for it. From that place of conflict with authority figures, she grew up feeling she had to prove her worth and value in life to anyone who had authority over her or who challenged her. It was rooted in her very means of survival. When she began to butt heads with the contractor, her unresolved wounds from the past flared up in living color.

This scenario begs the point that we can deny our past if we choose to do that. That is one strategy. That doesn't stop the past from having influence on us. We can hide, move thousands of miles away, and block it from our minds. That won't dissipate the energy. There are energy practices that can dissipate old energy from our being without ever speaking about it. Most people in our "prove it to me" culture and "if I don't see it I don't believe it" culture aren't open enough to access or learn those techniques. (I have offered one very potent technique in my free download on my Website, 30 Day Plan to Jumpstart Your Life.) Most often, what we have to do is look the energy square in the eye and say, "I am more powerful than you." That's when the energy dissipates. We can always tell where our unresolved pain lives by how we feel and how potent our reactions are in life. It's a perfect system.

I worked with Cassandra to help her see that it isn't what she does or doesn't do with the contractor that is ultimately important. It's how she manages her internal world and reactions to it. If she manages her internal world successfully, the external situation will resolve with much less effort—that is, abundantly. We cannot expect a positive outcome when the energy we use to resolve the experience is filled with chaos and pain. That's like making soup with dirt and spoiled milk, and expecting it will taste delicious.

Together we worked on her internal dialogue, specifically those things she tells herself are true about her worth and value. When the contractor called her authority into question, it caused her true belief about her value to expose itself. This is what caused her to become distressed and put her back in survival mode. She was reacting from past-time trauma. The contractor merely poked at an unresolved wound. He likely had no idea it had so much impact on her. For Cassandra, it was a wake-up call.

So many times when challenge comes upon us, we choose to only look at it as "this bad thing is happening." That's an egoic perspective. The ego says pleasure and comfort equals happiness. The soul says everything is abundant. Our ability to cultivate a birds-eye viewpoint and see that there is a purpose to what is happening is essential. It's really Abundance 101.

Until Cassandra or any of us can bring old hurts into balance, our abundant core power will seep out of us, rendering us half capable of creating benevolent outcomes. So long as any of us question our value, or the value in life experience, we reject the very abundance we seek.

Over a few months' time, Cassandra was able to see for herself how triggered she was by the past and decided to go into therapy. She found the courage to roll up her sleeves and begin the work of integrating these old habitual thoughts and wounds to bring peace to her life.

As with Cassandra, we are contending with the consciousness of the thing. There are universes within universes that exist in all of life. This is essentially why the answer to all of life's challenges resides in our ability to quiet ourselves internally and listen. When we listen, we can find our balance. Then our choices become clear.

The Energy Spectrum

In the Energy Game of life, it is 100 percent an inside game. If you master the inside game, success will follow on the external. It has to. It's simple math. When we get out of our own way and approach life from a balanced perspective, we find all the energy and inspiration we need to do the work of putting out energy to pull in energy. That's what meeting our dreams is about. Our dreams require a certain level of energy. We have to create that energy and put it into consciousness. It's all about the exchange.

As quantum physics demonstrates, thought precedes matter. What you think about something alters it. If we are still inside, full of love and trust for life, the only outcomes that are possible are benevolent. When we create peace internally, and that becomes the baseline of our creative process, all of our creations fulfill us.

In my view, the mechanics of the Energy Game flows on a spectrum. On one end of a spectrum you may have apathy, boredom, and depression. These are low-level, slow-moving frequencies. They are compacted in nature, meaning there is not a lot of space in them. When you create life or observe life from a compacted position, you set in motion a chain of momentums that will take you to a place of more contracted vibrations or limited outcomes. When I use the word *limited*, I intend to mean "without space." Space is really the magic word. When we are infused with space, there is room for new energy to come into our experience.

Conversely, on the other side of the spectrum, we have happiness, generosity, enthusiasm, and joy. Of course, everything else exists between these two polarities. On the side of the spectrum with happiness and generosity, we are working with high-level frequencies. They are very fast moving and filled with space. When we can create from this energy, we are always going to like what we experience on the other end of the momentum.

I consider "getting to the other side of a momentum" as a gestation period. Just like a pregnancy, it takes a period of time to grow a momentum and reach a birth of some kind. Your level of personal commitment, how awake you are to all the frequencies and forms of consciousness working in your life, and the consistency with which you "hold" high-level frequencies will determine the timing of your outcome.

One can see from this formula that taking care of the inside world is a full-time job. This is the task of living in a human body. It is the dance of duality on the planet. You don't really have time to worry about anyone else's shortcoming or flaws. The encouraging aspect to all of this is that when we manage ourselves abundantly and bring balance into our own lives, we can only bring balance to the world. Our journey is not just our own. We are impacting the whole at all times.

So many of us are fooled by the ego's perspective and erroneously believe that because we are just one person. we cannot make a difference in the world. Nothing is further from the truth. When we become the most authentic version of ourselves, we are fulfilling our divine objective on the planet. We can't do anything but make a difference.

When we take our attention off of others and stop comparing to the achievements of others, freedom becomes ours. You are not responsible for what other people do, say, or think. This perspective empowers others to become fully responsible. It urges them to continue their journey to authentic self. It is from a perspective of full and complete personal responsibility that people thrive in the highest ways possible. What people think of you is absolutely none of your business. Your job on this earth, in this human experience, is to be and do *you* to the best of your ability. In so doing, you become a force for love and peace. You set the bar for an empowered humanity.

Two Common Mistakes

When it comes to outcomes, there are two very common mistakes many people make.

Giving up on what you want

There is an idea out and about that an outcome needs to happen in a specific period of time. When it doesn't happen, people give up. This is an example of trying to force energy. Rather than adjust internally, to heal the impediment to receiving our outcome, or to cultivate a different strategy to get us to our outcome, we give up.

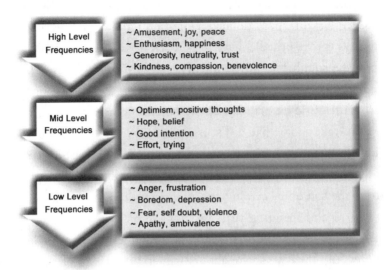

The skills we develop to realize our outcomes are what cause us to develop and grow. That growth and the internal message of "I did it" is what brings us happiness and makes us feel successful in life, not the outcome itself. The outcome is the frosting on the cake. I love frosting. The journey to the outcome is the cake. Long after the stimulation of the outcome has faded, the work you do to grow yourself is what you take with you and makes you feel proud and respect yourself in your life.

With mistake number one, I concede that there are moments we have deadlines and have to get from point A to point B in a specific time frame. I am referring to those projects, paths, and goals people have that matter to their heart.

I had a client, Gretchen, who called my radio show for a long time. She desperately wanted to start her own business. She had a solid entrepreneur mentality. One day I got a call from her on the air after I hadn't heard from her for some time. She said to me, "Phyllis, I am so excited and happy to share with you that I started my own business, and I am living my life's passion. I am just thrilled. I wanted to tell you that." Within the next breath she said, "but I do have a question today. That question is will my business thrive, or will I have to go back to another day job?" Thank goodness she couldn't see my reaction on the radio. My heart sunk a bit because it pains me when I see people give up on themselves, or further set such unrealistic expectations that they are forced to give up before success can take root. I had a discussion with her on the air. First it was practical. It takes any business, with rare exception, at least a year to get up and going. Typically between year two and three is when people begin to thrive. She had only been in her business four months. Then we talked about this idea of spending years of your life making someone else successful, but not being willing to work hard for a few years to make yourself successful. Then we spoke about energetic principles of success and how they take root, how we magnetize energy to ourselves.

Gretchen did keep going with her business. It did take her several years to begin to thrive. She did thrive. Ultimately, she was able to sell the original business she built and even positioned herself into another opportunity.

We have to be willing to face our fears and self-doubts and trust that life will support us in being abundant. When we are in alignment with those activities and feelings that make us "feel" like us, it's always the right choice.

When people embark on the life, the path, the practice of being awake in life, of learning to "allow" rather than "achieve," it is common to default to the ego's perspective until we have really mastered the art of it. Gretchen was the perfect example of how it happens.

Since childhood, many of us have been conditioned to quantify, qualify, and measure everything we do. We insist on imposing limitation upon our creations. We look at life through the small lens of the ego. The problem is that the ego is a limited form of consciousness. The ego is something designed to help us navigate the human experience in the confines of a finite human body. How do I feed myself? How can I fill out my tax form? How can I read this map? When it comes to answers from asking "How do I get happy?" "How do I find love?" "How do I connect to life purpose?" the ego does not have the capacity to answer these kinds of questions. It will always give us a lesser view of our capability, a smaller answer than what is truly possible. The ego does not understand "unlimited" form of consciousness. That is what each of us is ultimately. We are divine in nature, living a life that never ends. The body ends, but our soul's existence does not. You can't kill energy. It just changes into other forms. We must learn how to defer to the wisdom of the soul's eternal knowledge, rather than the perspective of an ego that was designed for a finite experience. When we do, life becomes a joyful adventure. This is the one key element in living a conscious life.

We attach to our outcomes

The second common mistake made in the abundance equation is that of attaching to our outcome. For example, someone may come to me and say, "I want to know if this XYZ job will come through. It's perfect for me. It's close to my home, I liked the person I would be working for, it's the role I've always wanted, and it's a bump up in salary. It's perfect for me. Will I get the job?" This question seems reasonably benign. What the person has actually done is try to sell me on the job to get a yes from me. It is normal and reasonable to want something to work out. When we attach ourselves to an outcome of any kind, and we judge it as good for us or not good for us, we have immediately projected energy into our outcome. We have interfered with our own creative process. We set ourselves up for disappointment. What we want to do is recognize when something is attractive to us, but not attach to whether or not it comes to pass. We want to cultivate a perspective that says "this or something more suited to my needs, or my highest good."

Again, we have multiple forms of consciousness at play in our lives. We tend to only look at the physical or emotional. "It's close to my house; it's more money; I like the boss." Perhaps the job itself is not right for the person. Or, perhaps the person is working on a different pattern spiritually.

31

When I look at someone's energy in a reading setting, I am looking at the soul's motivation and the motivation of the personality. I look to see if they match. Are the goals the same? The soul may not be interested in that particular job because the essence wants some form of expansion that is different than what that opportunity will offer.

The soul motivates the human experience, not the other way around. If we are blind to our soul's motivation and simply rely on the ego's perspective, we can miss some very critical elements in our own creative process and impede our ability to become abundant. We essentially drive blindfolded.

I teach people to cultivate the perspective "this or something better." I joke about it a bit, because throughout the course of my life, I have learned time and again that attaching to an outcome is a sure-fire way to make sure I don't get what I want. I have to consent to a complete state of "allowing" life to give me what is best for me. This is my karma. If I do not allow the intelligence that gave me life to determine my course, I am going to miss things. I'm going to choose situations that aren't really a match for me, especially if I am motivated emotionally. This doesn't mean I shouldn't work diligently or pursue things that I want or am interested in. It simply means I do not attach to the outcome. I do the process for the process, not for the outcome. In the state of present-moment grounding, the outcome I need always shows up. It often shows up far better than what I imagined.

I know *I cannot be given a learning experience I do not need.* The divine is not inefficient in this manner. The divine doesn't one day say "Hmmm...I have some time on my hands; I think I'll send a little chaos and challenge to Phyllis." Rather, when challenge comes I know it is an opportunity for me to expand. That's all I think. I may not yet understand the ramifications of my situation. I don't have to. I just have to keep moving forward in a state of trust and dedication. The outcome will take care of itself. This process is so much about being in the present moment, fully engaged in the process of expansion and balance, rather than achievement or an outcome or accumulation of a thing.

Expansion takes energy. It can be exhausting. Consider if you wanted to become an Olympic gold medal winner in a certain sport. You would have to train, prepare, and develop yourself to be able to master that level of proficiency. The same is true in the expansion game in any area you consider. It takes time, a gestation period, to develop the ability to even hold the outcome we say we want. A child may say "I want to be president someday." Certainly it's possible, but that child will have to move and expand a lot of energy.

In the expansion process, we are essentially creating space. Science teaches us that beyond the atoms and molecules that represent physical matter, 99 percent of everything is simply space. The more space we allow into our experience, the more room we have to allow something new in.

A different way to look at the creative process is this: Suppose you have an old broken-down car sitting in your garage and you want a new car. You are going to have to figure out a way to move the old car in order to make room for the new one. Whatever that step entails, each of us has to take it in order to receive our expanded good.

If someone wants a new relationship, they have to move out the old relationship, the old feelings, and heal the old resentments to be open to a fresh new love. Otherwise they may create a new relationship but will bring with it what we refer to as "baggage." How fun will that be? Not all baggage is bad. Emotionally charged baggage does not create peaceful and harmonious relationships.

The Energy Game is about intentionally directing our focus to choose which frequencies we are going to consume and align with as truthful or valuable. From everything I have seen, consciousness responds to feelings and potent thoughts. It does not differentiate between real and imagined. It is our ability to choose which frequencies we will run in our lives that can have an enormous impact on our outcomes. We have to act and behave as if what we want is already done.

I have a well-known friend, David, who tells a great story about his experience with leukemia. When the doctors diagnosed him, he simply went into his abundant process of telling himself, "I am well." As he went about his life, his children and loved ones started bringing him all kinds of information about coping with leukemia, including different strategies for living with leukemia. Although he knew they were doing this out of love, he posed this question to them: "What part of 'I'm well' don't you understand?" No matter what the external reality was showing him, he was going to define himself internally. He knows that internal well-being equals external well-being. Ultimately, he did heal from leukemia.

Years ago I had a mentor, Patricia, who lived in Italy. She helped me edit one of my books. It was more than an experience of correcting grammar, spelling, or organizing content. She helped me expand as a spiritual teacher. Our connection was very deep. One day on the phone, she let me know she had cancer. I immediately started blubbering and crying. I started going on about how sad I was that I couldn't come give her a hug. I had small children. I couldn't just jump on a plane and go to Italy to see her. While I was going on and on, in a moment she simply said, "Phyllis, stop!" I was taken aback. I thought I was expressing my love and concern for her. I was actually absorbed in my own reaction. She said, "If you want to help me, see me well. All your worry and concern doesn't help me." Essentially she was telling me in her own words to play the Energy Game with her. I never again took that position with her. Within seven months, she was healed from her cancer. In the first-person, I learned the value of "seeing someone well" as an approach toward supportive healing.

Life is going to throw us curve balls. We do contend with a human body. We all have genetic coding and programming from our families. We have karma. We absorb elements from our environment. The impact of some of those elements is known and some isn't. Whatever life throws at us, if we approach its resolution internally, we empower ourselves to receive the greatest power source and wisdom in this universe. Nothing trumps divine love and wisdom.

What I have discovered after more than 30 years of doing this work is that people are often emotion-addicted. I once was just as I described with my friend Patricia. We default to an emotional response. We are either happy or sad or somewhere in between when an outcome occurs we don't like. Most people go into the energy of judging, resisting, putting themselves down, or giving up, rather than using a different set of eyes with which to look at the situation.

Many of us are susceptible to programming from culture, family, and friends about what we should believe or think about what is possible in life. We are trained to respond to everything with emotionality. I love emotion. Emotion allows us to experience life in the human body with potency and fulfillment. It is not the only body of energy with which we can or should respond to life. Emotion is just one element of the human experience. What most people lack is a true understanding of their spiritual nature and how that translates energetically in the physical world. When more is required beyond the emotional reaction to life, many don't know what to do. When I talk about the Energy Game of life, it is to express spirituality in terms that a typical individual, perhaps even skeptic can understand. Once a person understands the concept, they can begin to practice being intentional with their energy rather than being reactive automatically in their responses.

I teach people the process of becoming intentional by expanding perspective and trying on tools that really work. Nothing convinces like tangible outcomes. That's what I love about playing the Energy Game. It works.

I have a saying: "Be amused. Be amused at not being amused." The point is to find your amusement. Amusement is one of the highest healing frequencies we can run in our energetic field. I use the phrase "insert frequencies medicinally." Similarly, if you had a headache, you might take an aspirin. If you are having an emotional or life ache, insert a high-level frequency into your personal space, and you will feel the effects of high-level frequencies in your outcomes. I typically use the phrase "imagine yourself bathing in these frequencies, as if they are showering down on you." Or just imagine a situation that causes you to smile or feel a happy feeling. It all works.

The phrase "Be amused at not being amused" is powerful. In a moment of extreme duress such as a death or loss, or being fired from your job, if you are able to crack up at yourself for your grimace or your messy hair or disheveled appearance, you are winning the abundance game. You refuse to identify in totality with the human experience as the only reality that has value. You don't have to like being fired or losing someone you love; that's not what we are doing here. You are not being asked to deny your experience. Rather, you are being asked to remain active in your experience. You are being asked to stop identification with the external reality as the ultimate truth. If you smile at your disheveled appearance or goofy smirk, you aren't appreciating being fired, you are taking care of your energy by doing something that will help you.

I wrote an article about six years ago entitled "10 Minutes a Day to Change Your Life." *(http://phyllisking.net/submnu-10-Minutes-a-Day -To.html)*. In this article, I describe the potency and power of medicinally inserting frequencies into your space for five minutes twice a day. It's not magic. It is miraculous. I ask people to practice this exercise a few minutes before they get out of bed and a few minutes before they drift off to sleep. Most people forget about it as it seems so benign. Within a day or two, everyone begins to notice things are shifting in their lives from out of nowhere.

I had a client, Barbara, in southern Oregon, who called me because of extreme depression. She told me she had been depressed for 30 years. I asked her to try this exercise. Within two days, she called and sent me a testimonial thanking me for the gift of this exercise. For the first time in decades, she felt happy and hopeful. Whether it was coincidence or timing, she shifted. Often enough, many of us make habits out of our responses to life. We are on auto pilot. We are not even aware that we are sabotaging our own efforts. For Barbara the act of becoming awake to her power and changing one thing in her daily practice caused the depression to lift. She was ready. If a pattern is simply habitual and we stop that habit, our life will change. We may not have to undergo years of therapy to get to a better place. If we do not know how powerful we are, many of us will abdicate to the status quo rather than simply take charge of our own energy.

This process of learning to intentionally manage energy in this way takes practice. Many of us have been behaving, thinking, and feeling out of habit. We have to develop a new muscle. This way of approaching our life becomes a habit over time and doesn't feel at all arduous. It is simply our new normal.

The ability to look at life as energy, as a situation with moving pieces, is a powerful position. From this position, we can begin to see all experiences in a neutral light, or a light that equalizes value. When we choose how we are going to identify ourselves in and to the life experience, we find more objectivity and greater power to create the life we desire.

CHAPTER 2

Birth

*"The two most important days in your life are the day
you are born and the day you find out why."*

—Mark Twain

B irth is a fascinating topic to consider. In this realm, we begin to discover layers of information and perspectives that many people take for granted or do not even know exist. Before a discussion of birth into the human experience can be had, the issue of cultural programming has to be opened. I use the word *programming* as a synonym for "filters." I do so to make the point that the filters through which we perceive life play a significant role in how we receive life, including the birth experience.

I have asked myself a "why" question for many years. That question is, Why does mainstream culture reject the potency of intangible realities? Culturally, when we consider intangible realities, we do so using the lens of the ego. If we broaden the lens through which we perceive life an intangible reality becomes visible. We can begin to more deeply explore our relationship to life and garner an understanding that enhances our existence in the human experience.

As I answered the "why" question to myself, I did so from many angles. I always find myself back to two basic premises: the first is that our identifications are so strong in the human experience, we cannot extricate ourselves from a perceived security the ego mind convinces us we have. The second is a potent fear to even try on an idea that veers away from our beliefs about what reality is or isn't, such as, "If you can't see it then it's not real," or "If science can't prove it, then there is no value." Simply stated, science hasn't caught up to the intricacy of universal consciousness. Fear and ego subtly—and sometimes not so subtly—persuade us to honor limited beliefs about life and possibility. Fear and ego are the blinders that reduce our options for abundance, happiness, and love on all levels. As we identify solely with an egoic perspective of life as the most valuable perspective, we become prisoners to it.

An illustration of this is demonstrated in modern American history. American culture, minus the culture of our indigenous people, was founded upon puritanical belief systems. We have been a society of rule-makers and rule-followers, even and especially when it comes to God and the intangible. God has been sold to us as something we should fear. Even more, if we question God, we could pay dearly for that questioning, including going to hell. People choose, rather defer to, a dominant perspective. This way, we blend in. We don't create waves or garner criticism or rejection. It fulfills our need for tribal connection.

In individual evolution, fear-based perspectives have a value to the individual. Yet in terms of understanding the totality of the life experience, rules and the structure of rules limit our awareness about what God is or isn't. An inherent rigidity pervades a "right and wrong" philosophy. That rigidity precludes us from accessing the abundance of information that is available through the art of listening with an open heart. We are unable to move away from judgments to allow a divine perspective in, and we reduce our ability to experience peace, access information, and recognize true purpose.

I do not presume to insist that everything I say is the absolute one and only truth. I do know for sure there is unlimited information available to any person who wants to allow it in. It is truly our ability to receive that is the variable.

I was born with a heightened awareness of a kind. It could not be drowned out. It could not be superseded by any philosophy or dogma that was suggested to me as a truth or a path. It over-rided my need for tribal connection. This is one of the things I bring to the human experience in this lifetime. I am not the only one to have ever shared a perspective about intangible existence. I have a unique connection to it, which allows me to offer unique insights about the totality of our existence. It is from that perspective of sharing and empowering others to be their best and happiest selves that I offer these viewpoints.

Life is on a continuum. Birth and death signify benchmarks in our evolution as any significant changes can in our experience. In the human experience, we graduate high school or college. We begin careers. We get married. We have children. We celebrate cyclical rituals to give rhythm and meaning to life. People we love die. We have health challenges, accidents, or surgeries. All of these types of events are benchmarks or markers that write on the slate of who we are and cause us to measure and define our experience. Spiritually, birth and death are simply benchmarks.

The challenge most people have with the idea of life as a continuum is that they don't have an adequate spiritual frame of reference to understand the concept of continuum. There is an inadequate understanding of our purpose in life spiritually. That includes our ability to see and understand the relevance of our experiences. Most often life is seen from a compartmentalized point of view. Finances are in one place, emotional well-being in another, love is another, and health is another, etc. Until we learn to see the interconnectedness of our life's journey, we cannot begin to grasp the idea of continuum. If life is seen as a series of stops and starts, there can be no recognition of a reality of cause and effect, or of life constantly creating itself.

As a professional intuitive, one part of my experience included a four-year training period at the Berkeley Psychic Institute. During one of the years at the institute, the training included looking in-depth at the patterns of birth and what was referred to as "baby beings." Specifically, we looked at:

1. Why we choose to come here.

2. How we pick our parents and our families, and why.

3. How we design our lives, and why.

Through the years in my private practice, now having looked at tens of thousands of people, I also notice:

1. How love is the dominant creative motivator in birth.

2. Why we reincarnate.

3. How groups (and even millions) of people consent to experiences.

4. Spirit has a sense of humor.

All the elements of these questions play a role in birth. Many of us can easily comprehend the idea of reincarnation, and that perhaps we "knew" someone before. Even if we don't ascribe to that philosophy, we can play with it and understand it.

Most of us recognize or can acknowledge that repetition is part of how we learn. We certainly know repetition is important for children. We have to teach and teach them again, until the information integrates into the body. The necessity of repetition is true for adults as well. With rare exceptions, most of us need to be shown, taught, or explained something multiple times before we fully grasp the concept and own it as ours. Logic tells me that the manner in which we learn, whether or not we are in a body form, is the same. We repeat experiences until we learn them.

In the physical life we know right now in America, we have free will and free choice. We consent to involve ourselves with certain people, to take on certain roles, to commit to certain acts, and to go certain places. Most of us have conscious and unconscious reasons for doing that. Essentially, we are free to choose our lives. Simply because our body is finite, and we change form when the body can no longer sustain itself, does not mean we no longer choose.

In physical life, when we have unresolved energy or emotion with someone we love or have had an interaction with, we can choose to resolve it or leave it unresolved. Whatever remains unresolved is what we carry forward with us. We either live with it or at some point choose to come back to the situation to grow it to another state of being. This is where reincarnation becomes a reasonable consideration in spiritual evolution.

Let's say you were married to someone 10 years ago and he or she betrayed you. Additionally, that person was extremely cruel to you, and perhaps abusive. Ultimately you found the situation to be too toxic for you to remain involved. Your response was to extricate yourself from the situation physically. You still had many feelings to contend with and bring into balance, such as:

1. Was it my fault?

2. Am I unlovable?

3. Can I trust anyone again?

4. Will I ever love again?

5. Will I be hurt again?

6. Can I stop loving this person even though he or she hurt me?

7. Are all men/women cheaters and abusers?

The physical interaction may have come to an end but enormous energy still lives inside of you, creating your experience. It creates through fear, perception, boundaries, and a level of openness. Spiritually, we in the human experience are here to resolve, expand, grow, and heal. Until we come to balance with any feelings that are not of the highest frequency, we will need to revisit and repeat experiences that cause us to understand our experience and feel peace. This is the inherent promise that exists in unending life. This is the road to enlightenment and eternal peace.

Any impediment to receiving love will organically want to become accessible to love. The abuser and the abused may want to incarnate repeatedly to dissipate a low-level frequency, or to at least continue to inch their way to higher frequencies.

In the reincarnation model, each time the essence brings increased understanding from a previous incarnation to the new incarnation, a healing is achieved incrementally. Sometimes there can be a full and complete healing. Other times, it can time multiple lifetimes to dissipate unresolved energies.

This brief explanation of the reincarnation process is one of the ways we are connected to birth and rebirth. It isn't the only way, but it represents one aspect of the idea.

Another way one can consider the birth purpose process can be illustrated through this example. Imagine the Beatles. This was a group who changed the entire direction of popular musical in modern times. I use the Beatles rather than Mozart or Beethoven because they are a group of people. It illustrates how entities collaborate and consent to the human experience to effect deep and powerful change, sometimes at the peril of their own well-being.

The Beatles had individual and collective purposes. They had to magnetize to one another on many levels. For instance, they each had to find a family that would allow them to discover their musical sensibility, or at the very least inspire feelings that required they explore their musical sensibilities. They each needed a family with a certain geographic location.

They each needed to find families that were compatible with their purpose. This required synchronicities on many levels. They knew before they incarnated to the planet they had a task to effect in musical history.

My dear friend Dannion Brinkley, who has one of the most profound near-death experiences on record and is also the *New York Times* bestselling author of *Saved by the Light*, has a great saying: "I believe in coincidence; I've just never seen one." The mind can reduce an event like the Beatles to "coincidence," yet psychically and energetically it represents the sophistication of the consciousness we live inside of. The intelligence that gives us life operates from frequencies of love and compassion. That helps each one of us orchestrate events and situations that not only expand our individual realities, but help us expand the collective reality.

The Beatles reference is a pleasant one. We can extend this to events we would consider horrific, such as the Holocaust or other acts of genocide. This type of reference can inspire great controversy. I am Jewish. In genocide, groups of souls collectively consent to experiences to affect consciousness on a greater level. Even those events we deem "horrific" inspire generations of healing, expansion, realignment, and reconstruction. The greater the need for the realignment on the planet, the greater the challenge or suffering in the human experience. It is the ego that says pleasure and comfort is good. The soul says "everything is abundant." It is when we look at life through the eyes of the soul that we find peace, purpose, and information.

I have a client named Beatrice who has one of the most severe cases of physical and emotional abuse I have ever personally seen. It began at the hands of her mother who was and is severely mentally disturbed. She is a person who appears to be a serial abuser, including killing and torturing animals, besides the issues with her children. For a number of reasons, she has flown under the radar much of her life and eluded prosecution. Some of this related to corruption and limited resources in law enforcement. At the time the abuse was occurring in her childhood, law enforcement did not have the tools or understanding to help Beatrice in her situation. Law enforcement tried to make Beatrice responsible or told her to "suck it up."

Beatrice's mother, among other acts, prostituted her daughter. The prostitution began after Beatrice's mother allowed her boyfriends to molest Beatrice, as young as six years old, for money. When Beatrice was a young teenager, she tried to get help from law enforcement. Not only would her mother not support her, she threatened her with violent retribution. The police were unable to put together any type of case. Until she became an adult, there was no relief for her.

Now in her early 50s, Beatrice continues to struggle with the effects of her victimization. Even though her mother is a frail 80-something woman, she is still completely intimidated by her. When I look at the patterns of this type of individual with this much suffering, it is clear to me that the essence wanted to again, or once again, experience victimization to completely understand the elements of the consciousness. The egoic perspective says "this is awful," "horrific," "sad." On the other side of the equation, Beatrice happens to be one of the most beautiful writers I have ever seen. She has a limited education, but an incredible use of language and imagery. She actually authored a book about prostitution, its effects, and the "johns" who use them. Through her victimization, she has been able to offer and contribute a creative story that gives an unrecognized and often maligned element—the underclass of society—a voice. Spiritually, I can see that Beatrice consented to an arduous physical experience in order to bring light to the underclass that likely helps many begin their own healing processes. Was her experience horrific or generous? Our perspective will tell us how to name it.

Whenever we think about birth or a newborn baby, we typically do so from the perspective of a precious little life that represents potential, abundance, and opportunity. We see the baby from a very vulnerable position. The baby cannot feed itself, take care of itself, or even move its body. Everything has to be learned. It needs complete care. The vulnerability of a baby causes most rational human beings to feel protective and to behave with tenderness and gentleness.

I would never contradict that approach toward care taking of a baby. It's exactly how I have taken care of my babies. This is the physical reality of a baby's body and experience. As with any person, we have multiple realities and dimensions that are working in our consciousness at any given point in time. Babies—more accurately I will refer to them as baby beings—are fully developed spiritual entities that choose to take on a body for the same purpose all spiritual entities do: to expand the consciousness of the soul or the "essence." Granted, even in spiritual terms, there are young souls, mature souls, old souls, and everything in between. Earth in general currently hosts a lot of mature souls. We are evolving into an old soul planet. That is one of the reasons for so much chaos on the planet. We are trying to solve it to make this place one of peace and joy. As we do that, we recognize our divinity.

The awareness of baby beings being fully developed spiritual entities is important. In the physical reality, we see babies as helpless and vulnerable. Baby beings are far from that. Yes they are physically vulnerable for a time. They are not energetically vulnerable. If there is any similarity to a baby being and physical baby, it is the relentless pursuit of getting its needs met. A baby can only see its own needs. A baby being has its entire awareness as a spiritual being and its greater individual and collective purpose as its motivation.

Baby beings are ready to incarnate. They have a purpose and a goal, and to begin to fulfill their goal, they must get here. In the context of getting here, as discussed previously, there are many elements that must align. It is through intention, love, and organic desire to expand individually and collectively that synchronistic alignment occurs through this perfect and magnificent system we call consciousness.

From all I know about how energy works and how the creative process of getting from the intangible to the tangible works, all choices are driven by the "highest good" motivation and love. "Highest good" means what causes any situation to elevate itself to another set of frequencies, challenges, or perspectives. It is not like the Jim Carey and Morgan Freeman movie, *Bruce Almighty*, in which God manages people and situations, one by one, through moral correctness. Although entertaining to watch, that is a limited view of how consciousness expands.

Consciousness expands through our intent to do so and by our own ability to integrate the divine perfection of each moment into our being and claim it as ours. This awareness is most easily achieved when we reside in a state of "allowing." We become peaceful, more loving, and more engaged with life in all ways. We recognize that the logistics of how life, relationships, and situations arrange is a synchronistic process of allowing life to create in the manner it already wants, which is in our highest and best interest.

When a being has a state of readiness to come into the physical experience, there are a number of elements I have watched throughout the years that appear to be consistent.

1. **We tend to birth into families with whom we share history.** There are experiences we want to acquire or contribute to in the family, or with specific family members that will cause us to hurt or heal. This is where the element of free will is so very potent. If we incarnate into a family that has abuse, we will be injured by that experience. To willingly consent to that experience is also an incredible expression of love. In a way, we are making a physical sacrifice in order to further the evolution of others. Once again, we have an individual goal and a collective goal. In this example, we can heal and grow despite the experience—or not. On the other side, our dynamic with the person who has inflicted pain has an opportunity to elevate from the experience.

2. **We choose a personality type and our talents.** Our soul, our essence has a structure to it, but it is fluid. We may be

creative in nature, healers by nature, teachers by nature, builders by nature, but in that context, we elect to have personalities to express in a specific lifetime. If we were to adopt a single personality type, we would limit our ability to expand and express ourselves. Rather, we take on personalities in a human body to learn the value of that personality in a specific experience. Often, baby beings will adopt a personality that one or both of the parents may really like, assuring birth.

If a baby being has selected you as an appropriate parent, it doesn't automatically mean you will have a baby. Sometimes parents aren't planning a family. The being is waiting around for an opportune moment to get in. Sometimes it looks a little bit like political lobbying. The baby being changes form, texture, or even gender to energetically convince the mother, or the couple, that having a baby is a good idea. Make no mistake: baby beings use opportunities such as when a woman forgets to practice birth control, to get into her energy. They are opportunistic.

3. **Love is present in all decisions to be born.** Not everyone wants to have a baby. Some people who have children are awful parents. It could have been unplanned or for a variety of reasons they are not suited to care for anyone. Even so, the baby being perhaps came into the experience to help the individual experience their own lack of empathy, caring, or struggle. There had to be a reason that person needed to acquire the experience. In this context, it is clear that it was an act of love for the baby being to consent to an experience knowing that it would not be a pleasant one. Rather it was selflessness designed to assist the person needing an experience with lack of empathy.

In other scenarios, couples, families, and siblings who love one another incarnate in the same family or situations that will cause them to be close friends. Most of us have people we refer to as "they aren't my blood family but they are like family to me." We find a way to support each other on this journey in the physical body. I believe that we meet very few people who have not been in our experience in some way at some time in the past.

Being born it isn't always about arduous learning as the path to growth and expansion. We may choose to incarnate in situations where we actively and openly rely upon love or comfort as the abiding forces in our life. The goal in the lifetime may actually be to reinforce that reality as dominant in our experience. Perhaps we need a breather from long periods of expansive lifetime experiences. Many of us know people who we would consider to be "born with a silver spoon" or who live a "charmed" life. Even charmed lives come with challenges.

I once knew a man, Charles, who was a millionaire many times over. His net worth was in the hundreds of millions. It was inherited money. He never had to work a job or consider how he would earn an income to survive. He had every amenity and comfort that life could offer. He had an addiction to cigarettes that he could not break. It drove him crazy. He had a deep level of distrust for most people. He felt their interest in him was driven by his wealth. Consequently, he had a very difficult time finding a partner. He could not trust that a woman would be interested in him for his personality and not his money. I advised him to seek out therapy. His self-worth was so low, I knew he would never be able to find love if he couldn't solve his own value dilemma.

There is a lot to be said for creating your own wealth and success. The process to the outcome builds your self-worth. It teaches you what you are made of, so that you really believe you are valuable, smart, capable, and creative. The universe mirrors your self-worth back to you.

I have had more than one client who had extraordinary wealth and did not have to work to survive or earn income. A bit like Charles, my client Miranda found herself focused on allergies pollutants, and becoming very OCD about every speck of dirt in her life. It precluded her from travel and staying in public lodging, even the most affluent villas and four-star accommodations. She had all the money she could want, but she was a prisoner in her life. Her OCD focus on the flaws of the external reality also precluded her from having loving relationships. Miranda also found herself in and out of therapy, struggling to find value in her life.

4. **A soul has a period of time for a "free pass."** The soul creates multiple exit opportunities before it incarnates. It is my view that all beings have a period of time within which they return to pure essence with no karmic implication. Most of it is up to roughly age 4, but some entities never plan to stay the full period of the natural lifetime. We craft multiple opportunities to exit the human experience. Those are chosen and determined before we incarnate. Life continues to have fluidity even after we have designed a basic template for our incarnate experience. We have to provide ourselves room to move in and out of the body if necessary.

If an essence comes into the body and decides once it is here that abuse or illness is too difficult to manage, they can choose an exit opportunity and not continue life. Or perhaps the experience is for the abuser or an essence who vibrates at a very high frequency, which can only tolerate being in this dense environment for a short period of time. They craft an early exit strategy. Or, if a parent was unsure about parenting and the motivations are not in alignment with soul-purpose lessons, the entity is essentially released from the contract. It can be referred to as a grace period, an opportunity to hit the "refresh" button on the creative process. Mostly, the implication is that we choose our death as well as our birth.

The term "exit opportunity" can show up in the form of car accidents, surgeries, illnesses, and violence (random or otherwise). Most of us have stories of loved ones or people we have known who were near death at one point. The person rallies and comes back to life stronger than before. That occurs when there is still some identification with unfinished business, if you will, that the essence wants to fulfill.

A friend of mine, Asha Praver, who is the spiritual director of Ananda, a worldwide spiritual community, tells a wonderful story about a woman who was very much a fashionista. Many people marveled at her clothes and her fashion sense. One day she was not feeling well and was coughing a lot. She obtained a prescription for a cough syrup medicine with codeine. She started sipping the codeine syrup early in the day and continued to sip it all day long. She wasn't giving any thought to the dosage she was consuming.

By the evening, she found herself back at her home, alone, overdosing. Rather than call 911, as she did not have the presence of mind to do so, she was able to crawl into the bathroom and splash water on her face. In her narcotic-induced state, she was thinking that water would revive her. Instead, she found herself crawling on the floor and holding onto to the toilet bowl. While she was hanging on to the toilet bowl, she began to see the tunnel of light, and began to go toward the light, perfectly at ease. She knew exactly what was happening. Suddenly, when she was about halfway into the light, she remembered she had an outfit on layaway. That attachment to the physical (her love of clothes) and that expression of energy had not been fulfilled. It was enough of a message to allow her to come back to life. When we have not finished certain attachments to various frequencies we will stay around for a while longer to do that.

After witnessing death through my clients' experience over and over and reading the energy of beings who have transitioned, I have seen a reoccurring theme. There is a period of time that all beings have within which they return to pure essence with no karmic implication. It varies from essence to essence. For instance, if an essence comes into the body and decides that the abuse or illness is too difficult to manage, they can choose an exit opportunity and not continue the life.

When I have connected to the essence of a deceased child, often they will share that the experience was too potent or that the objective they came to effect was not going to be possible. I liken this to the experience of someone who decides to go back to school, and they elect to take 18 or 20 units. Once they get into school and feel the pressure of the workload, they realize they are in over their heads. They find that what they thought it was going to be is vastly different than what they anticipated.

Another scenario I have seen more infrequently, but it does occur, is when there is a presence that is nearly angelic in frequency. When it incarnates into the human experience, the density of the experience is simply something they don't want to do. It's taking too much. They have already evolved beyond the necessity of this dense experience. They come in to shed light and bring space for a period of time and then leave.

This represents how free will always remains a constant. Destiny as we think of it, even the one we create for ourselves, is fluid. We can create, adjust, and re-create circumstances based upon new information—just like in the human experience. We may hold a position or point of view about some subject, and then we learn something new and change our position. We can do that spiritually as well. We have permission to do what feels right. If it feels right, it is right.

More than any other idea related to birth, the concept of continuum brings more of an expanded perspective than any other. When we recognize we are in a collaborative process with a consciousness that is a constant loving support toward the greater good of the individual and the collective, we don't have to take the human experience quite so seriously. This enables us to enjoy life more, trust life more, and allow a greater "flow" of divine consciousness.

Mostly my message on birth is this: we choose to come here. We have an individual purpose and a collective purpose. The dominant purpose is that which will expand the collective conscious. Our nature and mission is always to expand, to heal, and to become our best, happiest, and most loving selves. The opportunities we construct or co-construct with people and situations we come in contact with are always based upon love and the intent for goodness. We are all trying to navigate our way to enlightenment.

The human body, which vibrates in dense, slow frequencies, is a great method to integrate information. We really learn it when we do it slowly and with feeling. In the human experience, our desire to escape suffering often traps us from understanding the true meaning of our experience. We allow ourselves to be pulled into the egoic perspective that wants to measure everything in human terms. When we can grasp that there are multiple realities working in the life process, we can detach from external experience as the ultimate reality. Conversely, when we understand the soul is driving the human experience, we reconnect to our power and the infinite wisdom of the greater consciousness. This allows life to become a benevolent experience no matter what we are doing.

> *"I like flaws and feel more comfortable around people who have them. I myself am made entirely of flaws, stitched together with good intentions."*
> —AUGUSTEN BURROUGHS

CHAPTER 3

Death

"The number one cause of death on the planet is...birth!"
—DANNION BRINKLEY

The first question most people ask me is "When did you know you were psychic?" When I answer to myself, I would say 19 or 20, though my first memory of the intangible becoming tangible happened around age 5, when I saw formless shapes flying around my room. It was frightening. I remember feeling like it was more of a show or display. I did begin to sleep with the covers over my head after that time. I didn't question it. I didn't speak of it. I tucked it away.

In my elementary school years, I had my first experiences with what I now call "remote viewing" and spontaneous "out of body experience." I didn't know what they were called then. What I knew is that I could be in one place, and people I knew were in another. I would have an awareness of those people having specific conversations and consuming specific food. Within 30 minutes to an hour, I would unexpectedly find myself in person with the same people witnessing the exact experience I had already participated in. This didn't bother me, but my interest was piqued.

Again, I tucked it away and never spoke of it. When I was in my mid-teens, I began to have regular experiences with precognition, mostly through dream state. Most often I would have a dream about some event. Within 24 to 48 hours, the dream would come to pass. This again did not bother me, but I thought it curious. There were many reasons I never spoke about these occurrences. I kept them in my memory and didn't think I needed to do anything with them. All of this changed when I was 19.

An acquaintance of mine, who was in my circle of friends, died in a car accident. His name was Gary. Gary was a small, wiry boy with acne, but he had a very kind demeanor and a nice car for a 19-year-old. An occasion arose when I was invited to a special party at a local resort and I needed a date. I asked Gary to go with me. He generously agreed to come. He was happy to be with me and quite proud. My ego at the time was large. I thought nothing of "using" someone in this way, as I was not interested in him romantically or as a friend. At the time, I considered myself generous to allow this person to accompany me. Little did I know that in a very short period of time, this person with whom I gave so little consideration would open the door to my life's purpose.

One morning, about three months after Gary had died, I awoke to see him standing in my bedroom. He was present in a background of pink and orange. My immediate thought was "Did I sleep until sunset?" I rubbed my eyes to double check what I was seeing. As soon as I realized what was happening I became very afraid. My heart started pounding. My mind was racing and my adrenaline started running. At that same moment of being terrified a ghost was in my room, a "knowing" was placed in my awareness that life did not end with the body. Suddenly the entire idea of death shifted for me. I was raised in a devout Christian home, went to church every Sunday, and had a set of beliefs about what happens when we die. It did not include ghosts. In an instant, I had a "knowing" that life did not end with the body. Once you know something you can't "un-know" it. Knowing goes far beyond belief. It's like knowing your name, or how to breathe. You just know.

For the next decade of my life, the experience of "knowing" became a reoccurring experience. Throughout the 10 years that followed this event, my appetite to understand these intangible occurrences, and put meaning to them, took me many places. I involved myself in various courses, workshops, groups, processes, books, and experiences with healers, teachers, and anyone that might be able offer me a sliver of information that explained what was happening to me in my life. This period of intensive exploration became the foundation I built my life around. I didn't care and never cared about being psychic. I actually resisted that role. I was frantically searching for answers and needed to understand what was happening to me.

During this "searching" time, I had several awe-inspiring experiences that were truly miraculous: being able to see auras, intentionally going out of body, and experiencing a spontaneous healing event. However incredible those experiences were, the physical act of the intangible becoming tangible paled in comparison to the impact of knowing about unending life. Through these experiences, I was given the gift of a single glimpse, one profound sliver of information into the meaning of this vast and incredible universe. With that information came peace about the human life experience and death as we know it. It is this knowing of unending life that catapulted me onto a spiritual path and ultimately into the role I hold today.

With Gary's appearance, I knew in an instant that life did not have to be taken so seriously. Further, I could and should be fearless and live my life full-on. Playing it safe was an option, but not necessary. Ultimately I/we have nothing to lose and only experience to gain. Experience is the cornerstone of fulfillment. In that moment, I transformed from being a rather self-absorbed young woman into someone with an incredible sense of peace.

This transformation happened in a second. Then, Gary was gone. My fear pushed him back. In the moment, Gary looked great. He was in a tux, no longer skinny, and looked happy. He shared a moment of gratitude with me. Although I was not my best self with Gary during life, the encounter we had provided a deeper look into the truth and value of human interaction and our ultimate interconnectedness as souls. *It doesn't matter how well you know someone or even what you think of them. Any person can hold a key to your enlightenment at any moment in time. We all have the ability to be profound for each other.* This was Gary's gift to me.

For the next 14 years after Gary's appearance, no matter what I was doing in my life, I was in deep pursuit of my spiritual identity. I kept it separate from my mainstream life, but it was always dominant for me. Even though I started doing readings at age 20, I never called myself a psychic or saw myself becoming a professional psychic. I was just "doing" me in the world, and trying to understand who I was.

Today I describe my role in life as something that chose me. I am capable of filling many roles and doing so successfully. Being psychic or intuitive is more than a role. It is me. There is much more to my story. However, I share this piece of my history because my experience taught me that life is a continuum. Death of the body is more accurately a transition from one dimension to another dimension. All dimensions exist at the same time. Some of us have bodies some of us don't. Everything in life is amazingly and intrinsically connected. I offer the awareness of my personal experience to those struggling in life to help put a new frame of hope and trust around their own life experiences, including death.

The energy of death in a psychic reading is always fascinating. Different energies affect the reading. People will come to me hoping to connect to a specific person who has transitioned. Most often, people will come in with an expectation, likely learned from television or some other inaccurate source. Other times there is so much sadness, they don't know what to expect. They just come in hoping for relief, grasping at straws. One thing that significantly impacts all sessions is, once again, the Energy Game.

The physical body and experience is comprised of dense, slow-moving vibrations. When we no longer have a body and vibrate in a high-frequency reality, it can be a long way to travel to vibrate in this slow-frequency dimension with so much pain and limited awareness. Unless there is a reason or a strong pull for the loved one to come, their visit is usually short. They come in and offer what is needed and move on quickly. Most visits are short either way. It is difficult to maintain connection when the purpose for connection has been fulfilled.

A common question people ask me is why everyone in the family but them is having dreams about a departed family member. This is most often related to grief. The death is typically new. The person not having the "vision" or experience is still in too much pain. Grief is a dense and cloudy energy. The departed cannot be seen or experienced through the density of the grief. Another aspect to this problem is that the person not having the dream is usually trying so hard to connect, they close down their own receptivity by trying so hard. Awareness of the intangible reality is a "no effort" space. When we infuse the space with "effort," which is a contracted vibration, we close down the channel.

From my experience in this realm, our loved ones are almost always happy and joyous to have returned to pure essence where questions about life are answered. There is no reason to grieve or worry. Pure essence knows and sees the interconnectedness of all things, experiences, and people. Many times the departed are laughing, dancing, and busy. They wish that for us. A recurring message is "live your life, enjoy yourself, don't worry about me." Occasionally there may be an apology or an explanation for hurts exchanged in the lifetime, but most often it is a reassurance to the person still here in the physical that they are well, and that they still feel love and love each other. Sometimes there is a message of validation. Someone who has transitioned will show a picture to me of experiences they shared with the loved one, or conversations they had, or they talk about favorite activities they did together. This is always for reassurance and to offer relief. There is no "prove it" energy in these communications.

In the cases of people who die from horrific or sudden accidents, there can be a period of disorientation. The departed may speak of shock at the quick transition and not being quite ready to go. Even in those circumstances, they indicate they had choice over their death timing and when to exit the life experience.

As I have looked at this throughout the last 25 years, it appears that most people have at least four exit opportunities. That means they may come close to death four times, at least, in the life time. They can choose to come back during a life-threatening event and continue life, or exit. Most of the time with horrific and sudden accidents, the departed tells me they are content with the choice but they feel regret for abandoning his or her loved one. On occasion, they will report that they were tired, or that they only consented to be in this dimension for a limited period of time. Essentially, they never intended to be here long-term and served their time. This does not mean to suggest that being in the human experience is a "sentence" or "deployment." Rather, having a human experience is a way to expand consciousness in a very specific and slow method. It's arduous. What we learn here really "sticks" with us. When we fulfill our purpose, we take our experience with us to the collective consciousness. This allows the collective consciousness to continue to expand and grow. Everything is perfectly connected. Timing is perfect. Once purpose has been fulfilled, and those we need to impact have been, we are free to move on to our next step.

For those who transition by a health challenge, I hear multiple considerations from the departed. The most common story I hear is that the person was learning about unconditional self-love and wanted to teach it to others. Or, I hear that the experience was for others, not for the departed. The people left behind needed to expand in ways they otherwise would not have if their family member had not departed.

Other times, I am directed to look at longstanding genetic patterns in a family that come with karmic ties and other past-time programming. There are essentially family agreements to endure certain physical ailments in exchange for the family being together in the lifetime for various reasons. For example, a family of five entities agree to come into the experience to grow, love, and learn together. But the only formula that allows them into the experience at the same time is through a physiological system that has a deep genetic code and programming. The health condition for one or more people is unavoidable. Sometimes there is a past life or past time element that I will discuss in greater detail later.

I currently have a client who has suffered from breast cancer. Both her two sisters and her mother have suffered reoccurring breast cancer or ovarian cancer. The genetic line for this condition is pronounced. The agreements they have to share in the experience are also pronounced. In this family they are focused on loving each other and appreciating each other for the time and the moments they have together. They see one another as heroes in their stories. Their health challenges bond them together. It makes their love for one another more precious. In this family, the hardship and loss has been a connecting force and mechanism to experience deeper love.

In my view, there is no such thing as justice or fairness in the human experience. It is only when we look at life through the lens of an expanded perspective that we can flow with life rather than resist it or become angry at it. When we finally understand that the experiences we have are for our learning and growth, nothing more, we free ourselves from excessive pain and hardship in the human experience. We become more compassionate with ourselves and others.

Beyond mediumship and connecting to the departed as with any aspect of life, it is what we choose to identify with as "valuable" that causes us joy or pain. When we learn to equalize life's experiences, and see them from the soul's perspective (or the "higher" perspective), we can more readily separate from pain. We can then begin to recognize value in its totality. It is the identification with a "compartmentalized" point of view that causes pain.

In my own life, I lost twins in childbirth. I could describe that as one of the most painful experiences of my life. I no longer identify with it in that way. One may ask how I can see value in the death of my children. Let me say that one aspect of the process is that I have learned how to laugh at myself and how serious I can become when I sit in the energy of loss. I insert frequencies medicinally into my energy to alter my experience. Through time, I have garnered a perspective around the loss of my twins that brings me great joy. That joy would not be possible but for my experience of "loss." The loss spurred me on to develop other parts of myself that I might otherwise not have developed. Loss is a necessary part of living. Life is a constant flow of endings and beginnings. When we learn to flow with endings and beginnings without judgment or resistance, we become happier and remain open to receive pleasure.

I had a long struggle with infertility before I became pregnant with my twins. It was not pleasant. By the time my twins died, I was 100 percent clear that I was done with pregnancy. I had no interest any longer in being pregnant. However, in a very short period of time after the twins' death, I still wanted to be a mother. I moved into the process of adoption. I did indeed adopt a girl and a boy—the girl at birth, the boy when he was five weeks old. What I can say now is that I cannot fathom, nor do I want to imagine, my life never having known the children who are my children today. I would venture to say that had I not lost my twins, I would not have the same level of appreciation for the gift of parenthood that I do now. These two beings are my children, even if they did not come through my body. My daughter would have gone straight into foster care had I not adopted her. My son was also in precarious circumstances at the time I received him. Yes, in a sense, it was a rescue. They rescued me as well.

There is a tremendous perfection that occurs in the realignment of circumstances. We have to be open to it. If we are fixed on a specific outcome, and define it as "happy," we may preclude ourselves from the very happiness we seek. There is an amazing flow of abundance in life when you stay open to it. Often people close off to life after grief. I did not.

Within the same conversation, prosperity is also a shared experience. I was able to receive my abundance: motherhood; my children were able to receive their abundance: family; and society was able to be abundant as two orphans found homes. It is a beautiful marriage of souls. There is a perfection and synchronicity to all our life's events. We have to learn to honor life rather than resist it. This principle allows joy to flow in my life, and laughter to become possible. I surrendered to a wisdom that is greater than my identification with physical reality. That surrender paved the way for my greatest joy.

In my practice, I have had more than one family in my office with children who have committed suicide. I have had families in my office whose brothers and husbands have been murdered. When I connect to someone who has committed suicide, they are always relieved. They are always sorry too. Much of the session is spent reminding the loved one it wasn't their fault. Often these sessions are the most difficult. The essence tends to keep some of the pain they had in life. Mostly there is relief. Other times, they continue the discussion about why suicide was necessary in a new form.

With murder victims, often the victim will talk about the event and the passing. It is a sharing done with the intent to offer relief and connection to the loved one. It carries with it the same sudden death reactions of an accident. Typically in these situations, there are multiple agreements between the murdered and the murderer, and karmic knots that have been in place for extended periods of time. Many times the murder was avoidable. The murdered did not listen to their own instincts or guidance.

When families are left with so much unresolved energy, they often hang onto grief as if it is all they have left. They fear releasing the grief, as it is their only means of connection to their loved one. My job is to help people not only release grief but deepen their awareness of the interconnectedness of life. If I can give people a few moments of relief and a glimpse at a different reality, I feel I have done my job and performed the service I came here to deliver. I am fulfilling my life's purpose. The following story is an example of someone dealing with death.

One day on my radio show, a caller, Evelyn, came on the air. She was grieving the loss of her husband, who had passed away four years ago. She was holding on to the grief as a means of staying connected to her husband. Evelyn was also afraid of re-entering life alone. She was very stuck.

When she came on the air, she immediately said "I am struggling with a lot of sadness; I lost my husband." Before she could continue on with her "story" and reinforce her identification with grief, I said to her jokingly "Where did you lose him?" as if she had lost her keys. Many would consider this a controversial or callous statement. I knew in that moment if I had any chance of helping this woman, I had to almost shock her into a different perspective. I needed her attention. Right after the question of "Where did you lose him?" we talked about her situation and I suggested some options for her to try; by the end of the call, the woman felt relief and optimism for her future.

Later I received numerous emails from listeners who appreciated what happened on the air that day. Evelyn did indeed shift, and she became a long-term client and friend. She is now remarried. Had I not played the Energy Game with her, she might still very well be stuck. If I were to have just responded to her emotionally and said "I'm so sorry for your loss," I would have enabled her to continue on a path that was not serving her.

I'm certain many people will find this approach controversial in some way. The proof of its value is in the outcome. People heal and are helped when they approach their challenges energetically. Sometimes timing is everything. Evelyn had four years of grieving under her belt. She had a lot of time with her emotions. The timing was perfect for her to turn on the radio, hear me, call in, get on the air, and have the type of exchange we did. There are no accidents.

I play the Energy Game. I have watched it work time and time again in people's lives, including my own. The act of inserting high-level frequencies, especially humor, is tremendously healing, even if it is not politically correct. When we insert a frequency as if we were taking an Excedrin for a headache, it has the same impact whether the ego mind likes it or not, or approves of it or not.

Death can be a tricky subject to make light of. People take death extremely seriously. My goal is always to help people separate from identification with the physical reality as the total reality. In so doing, death and every other area of life becomes easier to manage. I lead through example, rather than forced opinions. I trust that people will separate from identifications in their own time as they are ready.

When people are ready to feel empowered and when they want to be happy, they will see that joy is a state of being available at all times. Each of us can choose at any time when to relinquish or claim our joy.

Death itself is simply a change in reality. Life does not end with the body. We come to the planet to grow, evolve, contribute, and learn. Within that lies our purpose. Once we fulfill our purpose, we return to pure essence. This is my message about death.

CHAPTER 4

Relationships

"If I love myself, I love you. If I love you, I love myself."

—Rumi

Relationships have changed more in the past 50 years than they have in the past 5,000 years. A study done in the 1960s posed the following question to women: if you were presented with a suitable man for marriage, whether you loved him or not, would you marry him? Seventy percent said yes. A similar recent study asked the same question. This time around, ninety percent said they would not.

We are no longer looking for someone who will help us with the mortgage and keep us safe. Now we are looking for a best friend, a soulmate, someone who shares our core values, and someone who will help us realize our core values and potentials. Often enough, the problem is that we have not evolved enough emotionally or spiritually to navigate this new relationship path successfully. Many of us still rely on old traditions, ideas, and programming while asking for the new model of "relationship." The following examples are various scenarios that exhibit this gap we are trying to close.

Most people think that psychics know everything. When speaking to us, many automatically think we see the totality of who they are in a second. This includes every aspect of their lives, from body weight to emotional state, to even their dead grandmother's favorite cat. Consequently, they will tell me *everything*! True, there are no secrets in consciousness. Unless and until someone asks me to look, I am completely uninterested in knowing someone's "business." I'm often surprised at how revealing people are because they assume I already know anyway. Callers on the radio are often the boldest. Perhaps it's the anonymity of the medium. They will knowingly and unknowingly reveal their most personal flaws without embarrassment or modesty.

Recently, on my radio show, "Sonia" called in and was very concerned about the status of her relationship with her on-again, off-again boyfriend, Brian. She quickly told me a story about plans they had made to go away together for a weekend. She told me he had called at the last minute to say he couldn't go and had to work. Sonia went on to say "... and I told him he was a big fat liar! Further that I had had it with him and we were through." Now, can you guess her question? It was "Is he going to call?"

Of course this is the ongoing question women have. "Is he going to call?" This call is quite typical and very telling of what is really going on. Sonia could not see the forest for the trees. She was demanding, diminishing, and controling with her partner. She felt she had the right to call him names and declare that their relationship was off over the phone, in that moment. There was no interaction. No negotiation. Just her yelling at him. Not once did it occur to her to express her truest emotion, which was disappointment. Even though she hadn't connected all those elements, after she "threw up" all over her partner and relieved her discomfort, what remained was her love for him and her desire to have him in her life. That's the reason she wanted him to call back.

Fortunately in this call, Sonia was open to hearing reality. I encouraged her to stop name-calling and to develop a style of communication that reflected her true feelings. For Sonia, it was disappointment. Like Sonia, many of us have to take a breath, step back, and say what is true in a mature manner, rather than project and expel our pain on to another person. Many of us become so absorbed in what we want that we forget to match our language with our behavior to inspire the best outcome. We have not resolved our own personal wounding, and we expect a partner to be our parent and make exceptions or excuses for our poor or immature behavior.

Women wonder why men run for the hills. They wonder why men don't return calls. Too often we generate entire stories in our minds about how things can or should be "if only." We forget to treat our partners like people, like the friends we actually want in our lives. Being human goes by the wayside. The only thing that matters is getting what we want. This is a very childlike and immature response pattern.

Women must to continue to learn the difference between power and control. We are the leaders in relationships. We set the tone, the pace, and the demeanor. Men want to please us and want to give us what we need. We teach men how to treat us by how we behave. If we are disrespectful, impatient, and demanding, we teach them that we are not loving partners. Women often believe they can talk a man into liking them. It is not through conversation that men find us appealing. We don't do it through conversation. It is through watching how we behave toward them that influences their attraction to us. If we are inviting, loving, and kind, they will find us appealing. This does not mean we should not require men to honor us in dating and courtship rituals. It means that women need to set the standard regarding what we truly want. Do we want controlling fear-based interactions? Do we want partnerships that reflect negotiation, mutual respect, and love? We should always measure our interactions by asking ourselves:

- "What would love do?"
- "How would love behave in this circumstance?"

In the questioning, we should ask it of ourselves.

- Is this relationship making me feel wonderful about myself?
- Do I like myself more when I interact with this person?
- Do I feel happy or anxious?

I have had the honor of teaching a Love Class for several years. In that time, I have taken hundreds of women through a process of self-discovery and connection to love. I find that women in general are amazingly sensitive, intuitive, loving, generous, and truly want real love. It is misinformation, programming from culture, and unresolved wounding that stands in the way of their ability to have love in their life. Once we address those factors, love comes in. It's not difficult. Love is everywhere. There are a lot of good men out there who want good women.

One element I have found to be the number-one indicator of whether or not a woman or a man will attract a partner is something I call *state of readiness. State of readiness* is probably the single largest necessary element to determine whether or not a person will attract a relationship. This includes emotional readiness, physical readiness, and spiritual readiness. When a person is ready, a partner will show up. It's the Energy Game. Simple math. The person we need and have intended to attract will show up.

From this viewpoint, a common difficult scenario arises when a man or woman is not in a state of readiness to be in a relationship yet desperately wants one. They erroneously believe a relationship is the answer to their inner angst. It is very common for people to deny the truth of their state of emotional readiness because they "want what they want." People resist pain or personal growth, and want a quick fix. They identify with a belief that says "I will be happy when I have a relationship." This foundation is doomed to produce limited results. When men and women hold this belief, they often settle for anyone that will fill the space. Then they set off on a course to try and change a person to become who they really want. The following story is a perfect example.

Sherry came to me for help with her relationships. Recently divorced after a 20-year marriage, she was very attractive, pleasant, and intelligent, and had a loving heart. However, she kept losing boyfriends two to three months into the courtship. She had no problem attracting men, she just couldn't keep them. I should also add that she had financial affluence and didn't need to have a job. This is a great position to have, however, some of my most challenging client cases have been those who have a lot of financial resources but no way of spending time that feels valuable to them. Sherry was one of these people.

Sherry is also the perfect example of someone who is not ready for a relationship but spends an enormous amount of time trying to create one and trying to make "non-matches" match. She took the courageous step to move out of a marriage that was clearly not working. When she finally extricated herself, she was hungry for connection. She began the re-opening of her heart without the important step of coming full circle on her marriage. What this means is that Sherry, or anyone, before moving into a new relationship, has to be able to answer the following questions completely:

1. Why did you choose your partner?

2. What were you working on to heal?

3. Why did it end?

4. What do you have gratitude for in this situation?

5. Have you forgiven your partner and yourself for mistakes and injuries that occurred?

Until we can understand the mental, emotional, and spiritual aspects of our past relationships and feel peaceful about all of it, we cannot move forward into a new relationship whole and complete.

Often, women and men say they want a person who has it all together. Inside of us, we have to have the very balance that we seek in others.

Otherwise, it is virtually impossible to connect with someone who has the balance we seek.

What happened next for Sherry is that she would meet men either online or at clubs. She was holding a mindset that her failed marriage was the primary source of her discontent. She had not yet taken the step to see her part in the marriage or understand all the elements of why it ended. It was simply all her ex-husband's fault. He was angry and controlling. She did not understand why she picked him.

When new men would come into the picture, she would start fantasizing about them and become very excited about them quickly. She would begin generating stories about why they were perfect for her and she for them. She was hungry for connection, so everyone looked good. I often describe this hunger similarly to my taste for hot dogs. I will never eat a hot dog. I just don't do it. They are gross to me. However, if I hadn't eaten for two to three weeks, if a hot dog were presented to me I would devour it. The same thing happens to people who are deprived emotionally. What we are typically attracted to when we are fresh out of a poor relationship is different than what we are attracted to when we are full and happy inside of ourselves. Sherry was finding everyone attractive.

Sherry's inner dialogue said that a relationship would make her feel better. Initially the men she met found her appealing and pursued her. However, Sherry began processing her life story out loud with each brand new person. She was looking for validation and a rescuer to reinforce the story that her husband was bad, she was good, and that it wasn't her fault the marriage failed. She viewed all her new potentials as soul mates immediately and shared every detail of her life with each of them.

This is the classic case of too much information, too soon. She couldn't stop herself. She didn't put it together that the men were captivated and attentive only as a means for a sexual encounter. At the beginning of a relationship, men and women will often put up with a lot more conversation than normal in order to get to the impending sexual encounter. As is the case with Sherry, these men would listen to her for hours on end at the beginning of the relationships. She would tell me how they spent 6, 8, 10 hours together just holding hands and talking.

Unbeknownst to her, she was the poster child for someone who has not yet healed from her life circumstances. It was apparent to everyone but her. Her dates could see she had a long way to go to be ready to be in a relationship, and that she was not going to have sex with them anytime soon. If she did, it was more trouble than it was worth. These men wanted to have a good time and get to know someone—however, not in 48 hours. Sherry wanted talk therapy from an adoring attentive rescuer.

In Sherry's, mind she was seeking connection and monogamy before sex. She wanted the whole package. What she wasn't aware of is that she was asking too much of a new person. She would not include the sexual component and put a lot of rules and boundaries in place at the onset of connection. Yet, she required enormous attention and investment from her suitors. She did not feel either safe or capable of managing a whole new relationship. She refused to be honest with herself about her state of readiness. As she was rejected by each suitor, she began to think something was wrong with her. The only thing wrong was that she had not yet come full circle in her own process to be emotionally available. The men she dated would quickly tire of her heavy emotional requirements.

Sherry called me three to four times a week for several months processing through her strategies and what she could do versus what she shouldn't do to regain men's attention after they disappeared. Slowly but surely, I helped her understand that men like to pursue women. If we take our time getting to know them, and allow the connection to build in a balanced way, many men will give women all their undivided attention. The interaction has to be balanced. We have to let it out a little bit at a time and stay away from fantasy thinking. We have to balance heavy emotional content with fun, and show interest and invest in the process as well. Men and women will give us what we need if we also give them what they need, which is most often love and acceptance with some form of physicality.

Although Sherry didn't want to have sex with her new partners, she would perform oral sex. When she began to feel her partners pulling away, she would justify the acts to herself as a way to give them pleasure and hopefully keep them interested. The opposite always happened. They disappeared every time. She sold them short by thinking oral sex was enough or the answer. The men felt guilty that she was performing for them, rather than having an exchange. The men, just like her, were looking for love and the whole package.

Women and men say they want a sensitive, caring, and well-rounded partner. If we don't present the same traits, those very people, who could potentially offer a great life to us, will not remain interested. A new relationship is not where we process our inner-most thoughts. Women especially need to process all that content with friends or a therapist as we go. By the time we have a new potential mate, it is about getting to know them, not using them for an emotional dumping ground or to fulfill some unrequited love quest.

I had to help Sherry understand that if a man is "into you," he will let you know. It will not be ambiguous. When we are in a state of readiness, it isn't a struggle to get to know someone. It's actually fun. There is no strategy. Each person is simply themselves.

Women are taught that men should have all the answers, be the leaders, provide financially for us, and have the highest skill in sexual prowess. Men love to serve a purpose and see how they contribute to our lives. They want to feel needed. Women who reach midlife or have already been married often need to update their information about men. Yes, men want sex, but they are not like 17-year-old hormone-driven kids who will stop at nothing to have sex. They want love and connection just like we do.

This leads into another common impediment women have to attracting love. I call it the "independent power woman syndrome." In my Love Class I often attract women who are powerful, successful, educated, and beautiful. They have it all together. They wonder why they can't attract a partner. Essentially, if we do not show we need a man, they will not want to be with us. Power women have to learn to balance the masculine "make it happen" energy with the "feminine" nurture and love energy. We have to learn how to shift in between the two frequencies.

Men need to understand how they fit in our lives. Powerful, independent women often hide their vulnerability and their femininity behind their masculine power structure that is their independent lives. Deborah brings home the point on the impediment of the independent woman.

Deborah had been working in city government for 25 years at the time we met. She was in a position of authority, well respected, and known for being fair and strong. Deborah was a petite woman with a beautiful face and smile, but she was also tough. She had been in an unsatisfactory marriage for a long period of time and sometimes the relationship was abusive. When she finally got out of it, she found herself with few tools for dating and evaluating new partners. She had survived her marriage but never really processed through it. Essentially, she jumped back into the dating game without any new information about her internal picking mechanism. Like Sherry, Deborah made this core mistake many women make. She didn't finalize the past before embarking on her future.

Deborah, like many women who come to me, did not have any difficulty attracting partners. She was beautiful, intelligent, and successful. However, she had two distinct challenges. She had trouble attracting quality men and men that were interested in long-term relationships.

In Deborah's job, one of her roles was to investigate situations with housing, child endangerment, and code enforcement. She had to run a lot of masculine energy. In her past marriage, she had to run masculine energy to protect herself. Again, I refer to masculine energy as "make it happen" energy or "take charge and get it done" energy. As Deborah felt the most confident in work "mode," she defaulted to running her masculine energy in her dating process. She would literally interrogate men.

When she didn't scare men off by her aggressive take-charge approach, her over-confidence blinded her to people who could see right through her protective façade and take advantage of her. Consequently, she attracted more than one partner who ended up being a scammer. Some people are skilled at recognizing vulnerability and using it against the person. Deborah paid one boyfriend's bills for almost three years before she learned she was one of 14 women he was dating.

With reference to running male energy, both men and women run masculine and feminine energy for different purposes at different times. It is healthy to do so. When it comes to general relationship dynamics women have to run the feminine and men need to run the masculine, at least at the beginning of the courtship while roles are being learned and defined. If we want a man to treat us like a woman, we have to let him be a man, and we have to be a woman running the feminine. Otherwise gender would be irrelevant. I see women time and again take over men's roles. They make men's decisions for them by planning everything and solving their problems. Women often won't give men the time or opportunity to do the things we want them to do. We're impatient and want what we want NOW!

I've watched women prepare resumes for men, loan them money, plan weekends, and even go out and shop for a wedding ring so he can propose. Our impatience gets in the way of allowing a willing partner to give us what we want. We emasculate men by solving their problems for them. We don't allow them to show us what they are made of or capable of doing. We don't allow them to be men. Men want to solve for us. They want to be the person who answers our need and helps us with our problems. We have to let them.

With Deborah, we began with small changes. I encouraged her to wear frilly lacey undergarments under her work uniform to send a subtle reminder to herself that she was indeed a "woman." (For a long period of time, her personal assistant called her "sir.") At first, Deborah felt it was a compliment. She was viewed as an authority figure in this typically male-dominated role. She felt she commanded respect. Bit by bit, she began to see subtle ways that she was edging out her feminine demeanor. She asked her assistant to stop calling her "sir," and to turn it into "ma'am."

Even though these are seemingly insignificant acts, each small shift sends a message about who we are to ourselves and to the world. It clarifies our intention to be a woman, to run the feminine, and to embrace our natural innate gifts as females.

There is nothing wrong with independence or running masculine energy. However, for powerful independent women, we need to know how to shift in and out of masculine energy to inspire loving relationships. When we learn to identify and intentionally shift from male to female energy, we will become successful in our relationships.

I worked with Deborah to remember to run feminine energy, and especially to run it when she was interacting with a man she was interested in. When I refer to feminine energy, I use it in the context of creative, nurturing, resourceful, and peaceful.

Women are natural peacemakers. We have an intuitive sensibility about creation. Our bodies create life. We simply know innately how to bring life and love to situations. When we honor our natural frequencies and simply sit in the spectrum of feminine frequencies, men love it. In this realm, they know their role. They know what to do. They know how to give to us. If we do everything for them, including running masculine energy, they lose both purpose and interest in our lives. They won't want to hang out with us.

Often I have to impress on women the importance of allowing a man to pursue them. The pursuit is what men love and what helps them define their own role. Yes, we can be encouraging, flirtatious, and put the dots close together so men can read our signals. When we take the pursuit away, men don't know who they are in the context of being in partnership with a woman. Women tend to be so eager to get the relationship going and to get to the commitment that they impose on a man's ability to pursue. When we take away a man's ability to win our hearts, they either lose interest or the roles become too fluid and undefined. We unintentionally interfere with the natural course of our happiness by getting in the way.

Women have to learn to manage anxiety, desperation, and desire to control so that we can allow men to be men. What I have watched repeatedly through the beauty and phenomenon of the independent woman is that we take away all the jobs and roles a man is defined by. Women hide their vulnerability behind the power of independence. They then become crushed when a man doesn't respond to their masculine façade. When we successfully navigate that balance, men love us easily.

Deborah being a quick study, and truly wanting love, really gave herself to the process of allowing the feminine to dominate her interactions with a man. One day at the end of the Love Class, she was lamenting about a moment during the week when she logged on to the internet to remove her online dating profile. The moment she logged on to discontinue her account, she had a message waiting for her. This man ultimately turned out to be everything she was hoping for in a partner. I love this story because, so often, right when we are ready to give up, our opportunity or our love arrives. In the Energy Game of life, it exhibits the perfection and synchronicity that occurs when we shift things internally just a bit. Everything else in the universe shifts when we do. This new man was someone who was retiring from the military and relocating to her area. They are now married. They have learned to balance the masculine and feminine in their lives. It was their ability to define their masculine and feminine roles from the beginning that caused them to connect emotionally. To encapsulate this section, let me list a few reminders:

- Good, loving, quality men do not want to be our therapists.
- Don't get too serious too fast. Take your time. Enjoy yourself.
- Be patient. A good relationship is worth waiting for.

I conclude this chapter highlighting another core mistake women make in the process of attracting love.

I had a very common call on my radio show recently from Tanya. Tanya called to tell me she had a date the next day with a new man. She went on to tell me his attributes as she knew them to be. Her question for me was "Is he the one?" That pretty much tells the story. Too often women are hyper-focused on getting to the finish line. Will I get married? Will he be the one? In this phone call, Tanya wanted to know if he was the one before they had even gone out on the first date. Where is the fun? Where is the enjoyment of discovering someone and learning if they are a match? Are we so afraid that we are unlovable that we have to know before we even begin?

So often men and women are focused on an outcome of some nature. We believe when a certain outcome has arrived, we will feel better, be happier, and enjoy our life more. It simply isn't true. It is our ability to be peaceful, happy, and full of love in the present moment, regardless of our circumstances, that determines our future happiness. The attachment and identification with "outcome thinking" is a stimulation that only provides momentary relief.

I have seen the next scenario many times as a professional psychic. Someone calls me and wants me to make a prediction. If it is a positive prediction, then they like it and hang on to it for dear life. This is part of why I have always continued to develop as a spiritual teacher. Too often I have watched people hang on to a prediction and stop doing the work in their own life. I recognized that a prediction can also be a death sentence to their expansion. I learned to explain energetic processes to people or the how and why a prediction will come to pass or not. The reader needs to continue the path they were on when they called me with full participation. Now when people like Tanya call my show, I require active participation on the air in their process before I will give them a prediction. I require they answer questions about their motivation and intention. Once they have done that, I give a prediction.

In Love Class, it is always interesting to watch how readily women sign up to find love. It is common to idealize "the one" who will rescue us from our loveless existence. Then about halfway through the class, when people begin to wake up to their programming, their wounding, and their expectations, many come to realize they are not even close to being ready for a relationship. In fact, there are other areas of their life they need and want to clean up before they will feel ready to bring in that perfect partner. This self-awareness and self-connection is very fulfilling. Suddenly they realize it isn't about a relationship with someone else; rather, life is about their relationship with themselves. This is one of the beauties of teaching the Love Class. When people engage with all parts of themselves, it becomes clear why they do or don't have a relationship, and exactly what they need to do to make it different for themselves. Love is a constant available at all times in the universal flow of energy. It is we who put up walls that impede love from coming in. Too often we forget that love also means self-love. We have to care about ourselves unconditionally. Once we learn to honor ourselves, respect ourselves, know ourselves, and heal ourselves, we can and will attract partners, friends, and people into our lives who will give us what we have learned to give ourselves.

CHAPTER 5

Life Purpose

If you're alive, there's a purpose for your life.

—RICK WARREN

Life purpose is the question we all have to ponder. Why am I here? What I am supposed to be doing or learning? This is the only question that really matters in the lifetime. Once we find that answer, all of our others questions fall into place. This doesn't mean helping others or being of service does not matter. Our contract, our agreement, our mission is to fulfill the purpose we were placed on this planet to fulfill. Perhaps it's service. Perhaps it's something else. No one person's contribution has more value than another. No one person's needs have more significance than any other. The ego's perspective will try to measure and qualify significance. The soul's agenda is to expand the greater collective. Each person's contribution is significant. It may not be recognized externally, but any contribution into consciousness creates a ripple effect.

If an individual does not realize their wholeness, the collective cannot be whole. It is a perfect system that works perfectly. The collective is all of us collectively evolving and emerging into our highest and best selves on a continuum to eventual enlightenment. That's where we all are going. Each of us is making a contribution to an ultimate higher state of being.

When we answer this question of purpose, all other life questions simply support our goals and help us further define our unique presence in the human experience. Life purpose connects us to everything. It connects us to ourselves, to love, to relationships, to career, and to personal growth. If we do not take the time, or show interest to know our purpose, abundance in all forms will elude us. Life will be a struggle without meaning. Our ability to understand our purpose gives our life context.

Beyond our need to contribute, life purpose correlates to finding love. If we do not know who we are and what we love, or are disconnected from the feelings/frequencies that make us feel most like who we are, how can a soulmate type ever find us? They won't recognize us because we aren't showing/resonating who we really are into consciousness. We are simply blending into everything else.

In the Energy Game of life, our "signal" will be too dim to be recognized by that essence that sees us as fantastic. We might as well be hiding under a rock. If we do not express the fullness of our purpose and really show ourselves energetically in the world, love will never find us. Or, we will find relationships we can exist in, but they won't fit well and they might be filled with struggle and discontent. Or, they will be short-term. Relationships become an arduous experience rather than a supportive and loving interaction.

There is not one right way to be in relationship. Those who choose enormous growth in a lifetime will often have many partners. Relationships are great mechanisms for growth. If we have a purpose that insists upon growth, we may be in a state of change at a more rapid pace than what is typical in culture. We do move from relationship to relationship.

Life purpose impacts everything else. Even with my own children, since they have been young, I have often said to them "figure out what you love, and what makes you happy, and then we'll figure out how you can make a living at it when you are a grown up." I am telling them from the get-go to think about what they love. Unfortunately, this is not a dominant theory. More likely, it is an opposite theory. People are lost in trying to pick what they "think" is the right direction, rather than what "feels" like the right direction. People are urged to choose practicality over creativity or heart-driven purpose. It doesn't have to be one or the other. It's a merging of all the best aspects of a dream to bring it to fruition.

It is in this "thinking" approach to what makes us happy that I hear stories that reflect a scarcity consciousness more than anything else. "It's not possible to make money doing what you love. I'll get a job and do my passion part time or later." That's fine. We have free will to spend our energy in any fashion we choose. In the Energy Game, what we love is our abundance. If we align with our highest frequency vibrations and exchange those with the greater consciousness, there is no way abundance will not find us. This is the ultimate abundant collaboration. The idea that choosing "money" and following purpose later makes good sense is erroneous. Perhaps earning money short-term as a means to fund your purpose makes sense. Purpose must be involved. Money is a frequency, like any other. If we give it more value than another frequency we are not in balance or seeing life clearly. We are identifying with something outside of us as abundant, rather than how we feel about ourselves or the fulfillment we actually enjoy from cultivating the emergence of our true self.

In my life story, before I officially became a professional psychic, I had worked in real estate, successfully; human resources, successfully; and non-profit, successfully. All the roles I assumed during that time fit who I was. They met my needs at the time. As with all people, my life is in a state of emerging. Each role took me a distance. It took me to my next challenge to master. Each role took me closer to myself. They took me to where I am now. During different periods of my professional life, I had romantic partners who fit who I was then. Often as I grew into other areas of my truth, those partnerships ended and new ones came in that were better suited to my more developed, truer, and evolved perception of myself.

I often joke with people who try to convince me that doing something other than what they love for work is a smart move. Why would anyone want to postpone reveling in their abundance or happiness? Rather "I'll do this miserable task for a time, and then when I have some spare moments I'll do something happy." That's crazy to me. Love and happiness are high frequency vibrations. They can only produce positivity. What really lives in that statement is a fear of inadequacy, attachment to external reality as the dominant reality, lack of confidence, fear of failure, fear of rejection, and fear of not having enough. That is the definition of a scarcity consciousness.

Modern-day culture does not teach us how to manage our internal world. It keeps pointing us to the external as the answer. Acquire more things. Achieve more status. Do more, be more, have more. Those external goals will never ever fill us up or make us feel happy. Most often it is the internal struggle, and the growth we go through, to realize purpose that causes our self-esteem and self-worth to go through the roof. When we allow the smallest vision of our self to be the common denominator we do what I call "small ourselves down," and life becomes a self-fulfilling prophecy that reflects less-than experiences. "I knew it wouldn't work out anyway."

I have many people who come to me in their late 30s, early 40s, and even early 50s. The following conversation with a client, Richard, illustrates this very common theme.

"I went to college and got a degree my parents thought would be good for me. I loved environmental studies, but we decided it was best to get a law degree. I got a great job, and the pay is wonderful. I hate my life. I keep asking myself, Is this all there is? I have money. I have a house. I have a family. I have peers who respect me, but I feel lost. I can't stop thinking about the environmental sciences. I still want to be there. Now I'm stuck because I need to pay for my kids' college and I have a mortgage." What's happened is the person went against their instincts and opted for the "mature" and "practical" path. They abdicated their passion and deferred to a measured choice of the ego. Perhaps the lesson of not feeling fulfilled in this lifetime is part of Richard's learning experience. Now in his late 40s, he has to figure out how to realign his entire life. It's quite a bit more challenging when you have a family, you're older, and you likely have less experience trusting your instincts.

I have had and have numerous clients with this challenge. I was recently interviewed by a women's magazine called *Unleash Your Voice*. One of the questions asked of me was, "What would you tell women now to do as young as they can?" My answer was "Figure out what you love and commit to it in your life as soon as possible."

When I became a professional psychic some 17 years ago, how I delivered myself was very different than how I deliver myself now, primarily because I constantly grow and I love creating new ways to express myself. I love learning and trying on different ideas. At the core of what I offer, I have always wanted to be of service to others. It has always mattered to me to show up in an authentic manner, and to be an interesting and safe place for others to land, regardless of my profession. This is how I behave in life. All the roles I held in my diverse professional background helped me to fulfill my need to serve and prepared me to serve even more in the role I have now. Even at the time when I was filling other roles, I knew they weren't forever. What was lacking for me was the ability to infuse spirituality. I knew at some point in my life I would have to give that to myself. It took time for me to give myself that permission.

Beyond my personal journey, my life has evolved into making other people successful, in whatever terms success means to them. When I do that, I feel the most like me. I feel completely in the zone, in alignment with what I came here to do. It's a feeling and an awareness of alignment.

When I began my practice at first, it was just to deliver intuitive readings and be present with my spiritual reality. In a short period of time, I began to find that readings alone were rather unfulfilling to me. Yes, I enjoyed being "spiritual" all the time, but it wasn't enough to read for people and tell them "Yes, you will get that job," or "No, you won't." Or, to tell them "This relationship will work out" or "It won't." I wanted to share with people why the answer was what it was, from all energetic angles I knew. It didn't feel fair or ethical to only reveal a yes or no. On occasion, a yes or no is absolutely acceptable. It's really rare. With the goal of explaining came the need to develop the language to be able to do so effectively. That took me some time to develop the vernacular that could be understood in everyday language.

I realized pretty quickly after I started my business that most often people didn't ask a question that would cause them to expand or think deeply. They would ask questions that were superficial or surface in nature. They were questions that would provide a temporary sense of relief or stimulation. Rather than asking, "Does he love me?" the question the person really needed to ask was, "Why don't I feel lovable?" "Does he love me?" masks a lack of confidence. If someone loves us, we know it. We feel it. It's not ambiguous. Most often when people ask that type of question, they are reaching, hoping, and desperate for a different reality than what they are experiencing.

I have watched people frame statements of self-doubt with leading questions trying to direct my answer in an effort to mask their fear, such as, "Do you think if I pull back some and don't pressure him, he will come around again?" It isn't that the question itself is irrelevant. But it's painfully obvious the person asking the question has very low self-esteem or self-worth. She is trying to negotiate for attention. I began to watch how people cover up and protect automatically. Their life trained them to do so. Many people have no idea they are even doing it. I wanted to free people from this disconnect I saw them having with themselves. They didn't need therapy. They need retraining in life skills. I became committed to helping people take off the blinders, shed the programming, and connect to their whole self.

Even more, I wanted to give people more than the information they already had. Most people come to psychics for validation of what their instincts are already telling them is true. Even if they ask me, "Does he love me?" they already know the answer. I wanted to go beyond the need for validation and give people a glimpse into the truer question that would actually forward their life. I wanted to offer an idea or perspective that perhaps they had never considered. I call this "moving people closer to their own truth." When we sit in the center of our own truth, we can hear and respond to our internal navigation. From that balanced and centered place, we make good decisions.

This idea of center and balance only happens when we integrate personality and essence. For years, I had a joke I told about trying to put myself out of business. My goal was to make people self-sufficient from me. For a long period of time, I wouldn't allow people to call me more than once every three months for psychic readings. Later I developed other programs to accommodate the need for support. The interaction became one of designed support to reach self-empowerment. Psychic reading is wonderful, but it doesn't necessarily cause anyone to become empowered. It stimulates the read-ee and gives them a glimpse into their broadest possibilities. It is when we take charge of our person and our life, and feel we can create the life we envision, that people are served.

As I embarked on this vision of service, I began to think about what had made a difference for me in my life. What helped me the most was an awareness of my spiritual purpose in life. I began to look at people energetically to see what they came here to accomplish in the life time. This became an integral part of my reading style and something I find extraordinarily fascinating to this day. It is a look into the deepest questions people need to ask themselves to connect to their life in an empowered and awakened state. This is the Holy Grail, in my view.

At the beginning, I had already been aware of patterns and geometric shapes that revealed themselves when I looked into people's energy. When I specifically looked for life purpose or, more accurately, soul's purpose, I became aware of what I now call a "blueprint." This is exactly what it sounds like. It looks like a schematic. If you were to look at architectural blueprints or blueprints of any kind, that is what our system looks like to me. The blueprint includes information about what we want to contribute, evolve beyond, and heal or experience in the lifetime. Within the blueprint, there are life themes, meaning that we have cycles within the blueprint that determine what we will focus on during various periods in our life. There are many variations. There are common themes as well. No two people are alike. That, in part, is what makes looking at a blueprint so fascinating.

Most people consider life purpose synonymous with a career or chosen profession. It can be that. There are absolutely areas of talent, interest, and desire that match us up divinely to roles that will cause us to become our best selves and offer the best of what we have. However, life purpose doesn't have to be career-related. It can be about personal development. For instance, people come to the lifetime to learn about leadership, to learn to follow, or be a scapegoat for a family. Or, they may come to learn about being ill or being a bully. Perhaps they want explore healing, empathy, or violence. Our purpose is not always collective or specific in the manner we expect from an egoic perspective.

We can have multiple purposes in one lifetime. When I look at someone's blueprint, it has multiple themes. Most people have two themes. Many have three. On occasion, I have seen four. There is a dominant structure and set of frequencies we each incarnate with. Yet, within that structure, there are cycles. The cycles or themes appear to be cumulative in nature, almost like graduation. When we have completed the learning or expansion of a certain theme, we move into the next. We carry forward the learning of our previous cycle into our next cycle.

One cycle or theme may be that of being the perfect child or the problem child. Another cycle may be to learn about integrity, or finances, or relationships, or to manage family commitments. Every person has a different rhythm and motivation to their purposes and their themes.

The only thing any person has to do to recognize their purpose at any given time in life is to pay attention to what is showing up in the moment. If there is a reoccurring issue with betrayal, job loss, or financial devastation, the purpose is always to evolve beyond those limitations. All the individual has to do is identify the feeling they have in the moment. Is the situation they are experiencing right now causing them to feel rejection? Abandonment? Power struggle? Fear? If we will quiet ourselves for a few moments, slow down, and feel, we can identify where we are in our cycle, and what we are trying to evolve beyond in a moment. As soon as we identify the dominant feeling we are having, that is our purpose. That is what we are supposed to be working on. That is the direction we should go in.

When it comes to career, and where we belong in life, the answer is always in what you love. The answer is always in those things, those activities you would do even if no one paid you to do them. Ninety-nine percent of the time, this is the direction a person needs to go in. When we follow what we love, it always takes us where we need to be, every single time. The impediment most people bump into is balancing the ego's need to quantify and measure the experience. It insists upon fixed time lines, fixed financial ideas, and fixed methods to achieve the outcome. When people hit up against their fixed programming, they can preclude themselves from allowing their purpose and passion into their life.

In terms of life purpose with regard to career, even those people who are working on emotions or personal growth levels have task agreements they want to fulfill. For instance, I may look at someone's energy who is a builder by nature. It doesn't mean they have to be a contractor. Perhaps they put technological structures in place for people or other systems that have to be built. Builders are often department heads or system programmers. One hundred years ago, there was no such thing. Or, a builder may actually be an architect or a builder of property of some sort. The person has to determine how to express that pattern. There are many ways they can do that.

I have seen many people who came in on a creative frequency. It doesn't always mean they will be artists or musicians. Rather, they have to always be in the process of making something new. They have to be crafting and molding energy all the time. Often these people are Web designers, artisans, or entrepreneurs of some sort. They may play music on the side or dabble in healing arts. They need fluidity.

If I see someone with a pioneer theme, this type of individual typically has to make a mark of some type. They may not necessarily leave a legacy, but they need to carve the path for others to experience life through their eyes. Or, they are truly pioneers of new technology, new ideas, or new inventions. Mostly pioneers need to carve a spot. It isn't necessary for them to garner fame or money. It is the drive to carve a path that is the goal. That is the purpose.

What can happen in the human experience is that we become confused by the noise of the external reality telling us how we are supposed to measure ourselves in life. We don't hear our signals. The advancements in technology have caused us to focus even more on the external reality as the dominant reality. The convenience of push button/voice command products everywhere separates us from our internal rhythm and navigation. These external stimulations can drown out the wisdom that tells us specifically what we need to do to realize our own fulfillment.

I talk to thousands of people every year in person, on the radio, and at live events. When people talk to me about career or life purpose, the first question I always ask is, "What do you love?" Even at this stage of my life, it is always surprising to me how many people do not know what they love. That isn't exactly true. As soon as I ask a couple of questions and insist the person remember a time they were connected to something that mattered to them, they do remember. They have been conditioned to push it far out of their awareness until they don't remember what they love at all. They are in a state of complete disconnect with their true self. Commonly, people turn their back on their purpose, their love, and their truest form of abundance. They allow the external reality to drown out their inner wisdom and guidance. They abdicate to a louder voice. Eventually the voice returns. Those are many of my clients in their 30s, 40s, and 50s who are now asking, somewhat desperately, "Is this all there is?"

One beautiful aspect of the work I do is that when people reconnect to their own truth and their own love, it is amazingly rewarding. There's nothing like watching a person emerge into their truth and honor the contributions they have to make in this realm. The texture of that exchange is powerful and gives me incredible optimism for the future.

Common Themes

There are many themes, and new themes do still reveal themselves to me at times. People can embody multiple themes. Or they have a dominant theme and evolve into other themes as the life progresses. Another aspect to themes is that, like all energy patterns, they fall in a spectrum. There are two polarities to each theme. Often each theme represents the gift and the challenge of the essence. The gift can often be how the person makes money or how they contribute to life. Or it can be how their express their uniqueness. The challenge is that part of the essence that needs to grow or heal or evolve in some way.

Some of the most common themes include:

- **Healer.** This type of person helps others improve. They are doctors, nurses, therapists, health practitioners, energy workers, drug rehabilitation counselors, and massage therapists. On the other side of the healer spectrum is often an ongoing pattern of self-abandoning. Healers must serve. They have in innate need to help others feel better. They often self-abandon. One aspect of their journey is learning how to show up for themselves as much as they do for others. There are a lot of healers on the planet right now. People who genuinely want to bring healing energy in its truest form.

- **Visionary.** This type of essence expresses itself as inventor or innovators. They are the Steve Jobs and Albert Einstein type of people who need to try new things. They often access genius or near-genius levels. In the opposite of the polarity, they often can feel inadequate or isolated because of their significant intellect or unique view of life.

- **Creative.** This essence can express itself as musicians, artists, actors, entrepreneurs, and comediennes. They must express through action and must move energy around in some way all the time. They often suffer depression, change roles and jobs often, and change relationships often. They have underlying discontent being in the body. It is dense and they want to soar.

- **Victim.** This essence expresses itself through creativity and nurturing. The victim is also self-sacrificing to an extreme. They deal with self-worth issues and struggle to have a right to live or have an opinion.

- **Leader.** This essence commonly finds themselves leading in the business community, but not always. They also want to be the ones to carry out instructions and make sure things get done correctly. They are achievers. They lead through charisma and strength of personality. Leaders also suffer from isolation and being inflexible. If forward progress isn't being made at all times, a leader can feel frustrated and without "purpose."

- **Scavenger:** With this essence, we often see it express itself through corruption, deception, and manipulation. These are often the people who commit crimes and identify with only getting their needs met, at whatever cost. The end always justifies the means. The other side of polarity is the expression of unmet needs. Most often, the physical life has either been abusive or neglectful on a deep level. The emptiness and feeling no self-value causes them to express without empathy or value toward others.

These are just examples of themes that emerge in a session or as one of many combinations of themes that emerge. Within these themes, I am able to tell where a person is in their own evolutionary pattern. Meaning, are they 50 percent through a pattern or more. Or, are they stuck, and not evolving past the theme? This does occur on occasion.

Although we are here to grow and evolve, expansion is exhausting. Our physical bodies can only integrate so much energy and information. Many elements can impact our ability to integrate. People can reach a limit and simply choose not to grow anymore. For example, to a typical thinker, no one would want to be in a "victim" pattern on purpose or for an extended period of time. Who would willingly choose to be treated in a less-than manner on an ongoing basis? Who wants to feel unworthy with no sense of permission to thrive? Some victims are unable to create enough separation from the identification to align with a different perspective about what's possible for them. Their abuse may have been so severe, they simply run out of energy to try to effect long-term change in their perspective. They only go as far as they can go. The familiarity of the pattern is something they can manage. They do. To navigate their way to a higher frequency takes a lot of energy. Sometimes they simply choose to live a lower quality existence.

When it comes to purpose, life purpose, soul purpose, and the reason for being here, there is no right or wrong about it. We set up a drawing, a schematic, of the ideal we would like to experience in the lifetime. Even if we don't experience everything, it really doesn't matter. We will deal with our frequencies at another time in another form. The nature of the soul is to evolve. If we take a breather, or slow down for a moment, it's all perfect and in divine order. Life is not a race. There is no finish line. Just a continuum.

— CHAPTER 6 —

Time

*"Five minutes are enough to dream a whole
life; that is how relative time is."*

—MARIO BENEDETTI

few of the most common phrases I hear from clients who are trying to expand their life in some way is "I ran out of time," "I don't have enough time," or "I can't make time for myself right now, something else has come up." There is always a version of a "not enough time" statement. No matter how it is expressed, they are all variations on the same theme. Essentially, something or someone outside of them is running their schedule. They are operating upon some belief in a limitation that insists upon a course of action or else a negative outcome will occur. It often lives in the "I have to" statements and the "I should" statements.

Granted, in everyday life, many of us hold jobs and must be accountable to our employer during a certain set of hours. The idea that we can't or shouldn't make room for ourselves in our lives is at the core of the schism. Energetically, if we cannot say yes to ourselves, the divine cannot either. We have to allow in what we say we want. That statement is the entire crux of abundance. We have to allow it.

What most people are trying to find in life is happiness. When the pursuit of happiness is found externally, it is always temporary. If we do not learn how to have a healthy relationship with our inner world, we distance ourselves from the one true source of unending happiness. That is in our relationship to ourselves and to our divine consciousness. This is what quantum physics refers to when suggesting that our observations influence our experiences. What we observe and then conclude about life shapes our experience. When we can master the internal conflict, the resistance to discomfort, we will be happy. Then, everything else in life is simply experience, without adjectives attached. We can choose to be joyful or happy at any time. All suffering is resistance in some form to the present moment.

Our ability to honor our natural rhythms is necessary in the abundance equation. If we reject self in lieu of an external requirement, we self-abandon and push ourselves away from what will bring us happiness. We set up a pattern of not giving ourselves what we want. Energetically, we tell divine consciousness, "Don't give me what I want." Consciousness responds perfectly by not giving us what we want. So our cycle begins and continues "less-than."

Any abundance created from a position of self-abandonment will be short-lived. That's why achievement-seeking always leaves us empty. We run ourselves ragged trying to please and achieve our way to feeling good by meeting these external markers.

I have a wonderful client named Jessica. She has been with me off and on for about four years. When she began with me, she was in her late 30s. Jessica is very knowledgeable about spirituality and extremely bright in general. She embodies the classic definition of a super-achiever. She fulfills a demanding role in the corporate world. When we first began working together, she was trying to determine whether to parent either through pregnancy or adoption. This was a contentious issue on many levels in her life. She had some physical issues which made it arduous. There was some question about whether her husband was really that interested in having children. We worked together for a period of time while she sorted through this potent issue.

At the beginning of our time together, Jessica had a difficult time acknowledging her right to have needs. She wasn't sure she was allowed to have needs or if they should influence her decisions. In life, she often deferred to her husband or the loudest voice in the room to avoid conflict. The decision to parent or not to parent was huge for her. Jessica wasn't sure she had the right to declare her needs to be a mother. She didn't know if she had the right to spend money on treatments to achieve pregnancy or adoption. She was trying to understand and balance her needs with the needs of her husband and the marriage. Jessica was very much in conflict about pregnancy and making waves in her marriage.

True to her analytical nature, we looked at all the pros and cons of her situation logically. In matters of the heart, with those things that make us happy, there is no logic. It just is. Jessica was too afraid of the potential repercussions to her marriage to make a decision in favor of pregnancy, which is what she really wanted. With full awareness of her options, Jessica stopped seeing me for a time to integrate her choice.

About two years later, Jessica returned to me with a new goal, but the same goal. In that time away, she had decided not to become a parent. After considering the repercussions to her marriage, she opted out. However, she did move her elderly mother and aunt into her house to care for them. I found it interesting that she became a caregiver to her mother and aunt, not to a child. She filled that need in some way. She was still able to maintain her role in her full-time corporate job and keep peace in her marriage.

When she returned to restart coaching, it was stated as "needing to turn her attention onto herself." It was a similar goal for different reasons. She was still trying to find out how she could get her own needs met in her life. She even stated, "It's time to turn the attention to myself."

As Jessica began to talk with me about her reasons for returning, it was as if I was talking to two people at once. Her essence and her ego were completely separate, not integrated at all. She was nearly out of her body sharing her thoughts from an analytical perspective, as if she were talking about someone else. There was no emotion present. It became even more pronounced as she began to talk about her deep sense of sadness from running herself ragged in an attempt to prove her worth to herself. She was so clear that what she was doing wasn't working for her. She couldn't stop the behaviors. It was a new version of the same conflict. Did she have a right to have her feelings or to express them? Her feelings didn't line up on the spreadsheet of her life plan. That's the way it was, and somehow she had to make peace with it. She was very sad, but not able to feel her sadness. She could only talk about it as if it were some else.

Although she seemed to have made peace with her parenting choice, the internal conflict of "am I allowed to have my needs met" had transferred to a topic that was more palatable to the people in her life. There was no conflict with her husband around caring for her aging mother and aunt, or for her to take a class or do some coaching. Jessica's family also brought financial resources into the home. Her husband was very financially concerned. She was in a safe and protected place to once again peel back the layers of her perspective.

After we spoke, we set up a time to restart her sessions, about three weeks in the future. (Typically, when people are ready to feel differently, they want to begin to feel differently right away, so this was a little unusual.) Jessica had her reasons for starting several weeks later, so I honored her rhythm. The day before her appointment, I received an email from Jessica saying her boss scheduled a last-minute meeting and she had to go into the office, so we would need to reschedule our appointment. We did so for the following week. I wondered if she was going to keep the appointment. Sometimes these delay tactics represent a resistance to change and an inability to put oneself first.

The following week Jessica did keep her appointment. I didn't bring up to her whether or not she had set her needs to the side in lieu of her boss's last minute call for a meeting. I didn't know how critical the meeting was or wasn't. I just tucked the thoughts away to watch what would happen next.

In our first appointment, it didn't take long for us to get to her core issue of feeling a lack of permission to do what she needed to do for herself, and how she still feels she needs to earn approval from others to feel valuable in life. She had created a momentum in her life that she was unable to stop, even though she wanted to stop. Most everyone in her life had come to know her as the "get it done" person. She was the person who could manage anything. She had essentially trained everyone in her life to expect enormous things from her and to be a "giver" in their life. Now, as she wanted to change that dynamic and begin to do less, she couldn't make it happen, and she even questioned if it were possible. There was a low-level sense of desperation in her voice.

I gave her an assignment to begin in small ways to make room for herself in her life, and to begin to bring her spiritual principles into her everyday life. Jessica would spend an hour a day every night reading, listening to spiritual radio shows, or doing some form of meditation. It was only for her in the privacy of her bedroom. Once she left that room, her spiritual principles disappeared.

We began to discuss this idea of living two lives (meaning a life that excluded the wealth of her spiritual awareness) and why she did that. We wanted to discover how she could begin to integrate the principles she holds so dear into her everyday life. Why have a frame for navigating the life experience if you aren't going to apply it? As she began to answer that question to herself, we kept finding our way back to: "I don't deserve," "I don't want to be judged," and "I want to be part of my tribe." Part of our work together was to help her bridge the gap, the fears, and the conditioning that said it was to be one way or the other.

Jessica also mentioned that she was very down on herself about her weight. She felt she was overweight and criticized herself relentlessly. She viewed herself as "less than" because she believed she had extra weight on her body. Excess weight always indicates that we are "holding on" to energy that needs to be released. She clearly was holding on to the energy of "I am less than and not worthy." She needed to hold on to energy because she was constantly giving in an effort to be liked or seen as valuable. We have to draw on energy from somewhere. The idea that we have to be perpetual givers feeds the idea that we have to achieve our way to feeling good. It's a bottom less pit.

I asked Jessica to consider how her extra weight served her. Not why it was wrong in her life, but why it was right. I asked her to find meaning in why she allowed the extra weight but also to acknowledge how her body consistently responded perfectly to her requests. I asked her to honor her body for being such an amazing friend to her. I asked her to remind herself her body was doing what she was asking, and to cultivate a sense of appreciation for the perfection in that relationship. I encouraged her to honor her body, not put it down. Finally, I asked her to write about her inner beliefs about why she didn't deserve to feel good about herself and about how she has abandoned herself and to forgive herself for that act.

The key to this process is to recognize its value and honor it. That is the key in all forms of abundance. Once we recognize the value, we can shift. So long as we resist, the situation we don't like persists.

Another principle for Jessica was that of increasing space in her day. She was always tired, worn from going from here to there, and feeling depleted. I talked with her about being the master of her own creative rhythms, and to allow life to adjust around the rhythms she determined were right for her. When Jessica was contemplating pregnancy, the idea of choosing what she wanted and allowing the rhythms to adjust around her were too vast. It could have potentially signaled the end of her marriage. That was too much for her. In these circumstances, they were safe enough to her that we were able to begin a process.

I also asked her to use "choose" language rather than "have to" language. The energy of "I choose to do this thing," feels very different than

"I have to do this thing." Jessica made great progress in her awareness in this session. I sat back to watch what would happen next.

The day before our next scheduled appointment, I received an email from Jessica. Once again she indicated that work was coming in between her and our appointment. Then she indicated that with the holidays and other things, it would likely be three weeks before we could speak again. She proposed a date three weeks in the future. I empower my clients to determine when they want to see me and what works for their schedule. However, this rescheduling was too coincidental for my comfort level. After a two-week break, most people lose momentum and have to start all over again. I felt I had to bring to her attention that it wasn't that she wasn't showing up for me. She wasn't showing up for herself. I explained that three weeks is really too much time in between sessions if she is to continue to make progress. I even went as far as to give her a weekend option so that work could not interfere with her schedule.

Interestingly, Jessica agreed to make time in just three days. I didn't have to go any further with her self-abandoning; rather, I just had to remind her what works in processes of change.

For Jessica, as with all people, we have to retrain ourselves. We are indeed creatures of habit. In Jessica's mind, she absolutely wanted to change. She was exhausted. She had so many habits in place. Change doesn't come naturally for any of us. That's why support is so beneficial. If we have a buddy, a coach, or someone who can remind us to stay awake to what matters to us, it helps. After we have made habits out of patterns over long periods of time, we don't even realize what we are doing to ourselves.

When Jessica and I spoke three days later, it was an amazing conversation. Her boss had essentially asked her to take on a number of projects for him. Rather than consent without thinking and pressing forward in an effort to please, as she would typically do, she elected to say nothing. She went to the privacy of her own space and decided to consider what would actually work for her in her life to maintain balance.

Jessica realized that she would be able to take on one or two of the projects but not all of them. If she took on everything, she would become overwhelmed, and once again have no room for herself in her own life. She noticed that a couple of the projects were not in her area of expertise. They would require even more of her time and energy. She crafted a strategy to explain to her boss why he should delegate the additional projects to a different department, as that department had a higher level of expertise than she did. Jessica was able to give him a resource at the same time she was saying no. "No" was not a word she was accustomed to using. While she shared her process, it was fascinating to watch her resistance to her own process. On one hand, she was absolutely relieved to say no to the excessive work request. On the other hand, she was terrified she may be rejected or condemned in some way. Her approach in the workplace environment had always been to do 110 percent, and to go above and beyond what was asked. She had become acutely aware that her insistence upon doing more than necessary was not about excellence or doing a good job. She was being driven by a need to feel worthy. She did not have to match her boss's drive to climb the corporate ladder and take that on as her own. If he wanted to do excessive work and projects, he could. That was not part of her goals or her job requirements.

When she finally relayed her answer and suggestions to her boss, he accepted them. He didn't jump for joy, but that's okay. Jessica was creating balance, and learning to honor herself. That activity will always and only bring us into alignment with our truest and highest potential.

The wonderful Miguel Ruiz, author of *The Four Agreements,* wrote "Always do your best." This is one of the four agreements. Yet, doing your best is not doing more than you should and can in a given moment. If you are taking yourself out of balance, you are not doing your best.

Jessica's awareness of her pattern of going out of balance, coupled with the fatigue of driving herself relentlessly, was forcing her to reach for change. It was not without a different discomfort. This was new territory for her. Even *good* new feelings can make us feel awkward. Jessica was now inch by inch beginning to face the emptiness she felt inside and its causes.

How We Identify With Time

The human body is finite. It has a beginning, a middle, and an end. The physical world speaks to us in terms of a beginning, middle, and end. It seeks to quantify, qualify, and measure everything to fit into the model and the structure in a way the ego mind can comprehend.

In reality, time is an illusion. This is easy to say, not as easy to understand, until we break it down. Time is something the finite awareness uses to define itself. The essence, our soul, is timeless and knows no limitation or boundary, and needs no point of reference. It just is, always has been and always will be.

When we cease identification with experiences as good, bad, right, wrong, important, or not important, we cease the need to measure time. We become interested observers. We simply see the value of our role in existence at a particular moment in life. As I was writing this time piece, I received a phone call from a dear friend. She was telling me how her car engine had blown up. She and her husband both ignored the signs the car had given them, including the "check engine" light. Now they were faced with having to buy a new car. The car she was talking about was 10 years old. It had enormous wear and tear.

I listened compassionately to my friend. I couldn't help but notice all the adjectives she attached to measure her experience: "This is so terrible." This is not what I want to spend my money on right now. I just don't want to deal with this."

This scenario beautifully illustrated how most of us react when something doesn't go the way we want it to go. We plan and organize our lives to go a certain way. We set up both simple and elaborate systems to implement the outcomes we want. We want to execute those strategies for our perfect and benevolent life. Then life throws us a curve we hadn't factored into our process. We forget that we are part of something greater than ourselves. We can't control everything. It is in how we learn to flow with life's curveballs that we find peace.

I said to my friend lovingly, "At least you have the money to spend on a car." She said "You're right. That's true. I just wanted to spend it on other things." My friend was so frustrated in the moment, she wasn't able to grab the bird's eye view and acknowledge that she had 10 years of great service from her car. She had gone years without a car payment. Nothing lasts forever. Even in this mundane example, my friend had to work her way through her own resistance to modify her plans. Much of her resistance was about going into a dealership to face the arduous process of buying a car and all that entails. Her husband did elect to take that chore off her hands. In a few days' time, she will have a new car. She will begin to remember all the flaws and problems that existed with the older car that she had overlooked because it suited her current needs. She will begin to see why having the new car is a beneficial thing for her.

This mundane situation illustrates the typical pattern most of us follow to varying degrees. We lament and resist life, and then eventually come to a place of acceptance. If we are determined, we will find happiness in our new circumstances. The quicker we can navigate these cycles and go straight to acceptance and happiness, the more happiness we will have. It is our resistance to our own discomfort, our own beliefs about what needs to occur, that cause us distress.

The use of time is what we do to define ourselves in physical life. It imposes and insists value on what we do. In the human experience, we do have to meet deadlines and cooperate in such a way that encourages a functional society. If we seek happiness we must commit to:

1. Honor peace.

2. Embrace surrender.

3. Eradicate resistance from our response patterns.

We have to train ourselves to accept each moment with gratitude and appreciation. If we allow every moment to be exactly what it is without judgment, we fulfill our spiritual need, which is exponentially greater than the need of our human body.

We are not on our way to somewhere or trying to achieve anything. We are existing and expanding through experience. We are already where we need to be in each moment. When we consent to this truth about the purpose of being in a body on the planet, the only experience we can have or create is abundance.

Time imposes judgments such as:

1. Am I too old?

2. Am I too young?

3. Am I too fat?

4. Are my grades good enough?

5. Do I have enough time?

6. Am I rushed?

7. Is there enough time in the day?

Ultimately, each of us sets the rhythm and momentum of our life. We choose where to place our attention and how to spend our energy. When time is the master, we diminish our own power to create or to experience magnificence. We relinquish power and autonomy in our own world.

If we identify with past wounding, or past programming, we are living in the past. If we are waiting for our "good" to arrive, we are living in a future reality. Yet, if we are in the present moment unattached and unidentified with experiences through judgment, time becomes irrelevant. We are simply observing expansion and participating in it. We focus only on being present. Being present in the moment without judgment, identification, or attachment equals happiness.

In this life, the purpose for being here is to elevate and expand our consciousness. What does that really mean? It means that we are resolving, completing, adding to, enjoying, and learning how to manage energy in such a way that we can exist in higher realms. It is common for people to say they want more happiness, more money, more love, and simply more of everything. What is not common is when people are willing to consent to the ideas or activities that will cause them to be receptacles for these things.

I can begin with a very basic example. People often come to me to help them increase their income and grow their businesses. I will give them three to five specific "to-do" items. These are necessary steps any business has to take to build and grow income. The client doesn't do the steps. When I get into their reasons why they didn't do it, it's very similar to the story of Jessica in that they often don't believe they deserve abundance, or they are afraid of success or failure. They choose to do nothing, and offer many excuses for why they aren't taking the steps.

As we dissect this type of scenario, we can see that the individual has to heal from their low self-worth. That action is one of abundance. We tend to think abundance is only money. Every vibration we bring into balance allows us to receive more. We have to do our part in the contribution/exchange relationship to receive the good things we say we want. This is the life. We are here to raise our frequencies so that we can enjoy more and more divinity. We have to consent to it. It is our choice in each moment whether we consent to or deny abundance.

We hear the statement that time is an illusion, and that the past, present, and future all exist at the same time—even though it is always *now* whenever we are speaking. When you are reading this book 10 minutes from now, it will still be *now*. The idea that time is illusory is difficult to grasp unless you have some belief that reincarnation exists, or at the very least, we are going somewhere from where we are now.

Reincarnation

Through time, I have become more persuaded about the existence of reincarnation, especially when I see a child prodigy on TV or on YouTube who sings like a mature individual, even though they are 8 or 9 years old. A knowing sets in that they had to have been accomplished in another time. When they left the body in that incarnation, they said to themselves "I am not going to forget all of the work and development of this lifetime."

There are also people who have been significant in my life. I have had a sense of "knowing" them the moment I met them. A familiarity existed. I was extraordinarily drawn to them more than other people. Although everything is in the now, in our energy centers, our chakras, we carry forward all the information from all the experiences we have ever had. Although something may have happened 300 years ago, if it wasn't resolved to the highest frequency, we will be drawn to it. Or if we had a particularly good time with someone, we will recognize them energetically and be drawn to them. It may not be a conscious recognition, but we will move forward with them through some other rational explanation.

I had an experience with a first love when I was 18. The moment I laid eyes on him and felt his presence, I had never been so drawn to a person. I just thought it was because he was cute. At least, he was cute to me. We became involved in a passionate and intense love affair. About a year into it, I began to learn and experience that he was quite deceptive and cruel. He turned out to be the opposite of what I believed he was. I was extremely devastated by the experience.

Later, after a debilitating breakup, I happened upon a book entitled *You Were Born Again to Be Together*. This book gave me my first glimpse into the idea of reincarnation. The book provided case studies that were very compelling. It was a completely new idea to me. I was so stimulated by the idea, I wanted to experience past-life regression personally. I found a class in Berkeley, California, and began a 16-week course in past-life regression.

When I went through the past life regression course I discovered a lifetime with my ex-boyfriend where we had been married. In that lifetime, he was very cruel and controlling. He would not even allow me to leave the house. I had a miserable life. We lived in a remote area. I was practically a prisoner. There was no transportation in that era. In that lifetime, I had no options. In this lifetime, I was able to get away from him. Granted, I loved him and wanted our romance, but I did not want to resign myself to abuse or cruelty. When the cruelty began, I was able to extricate myself from it.

There was progress between lifetimes. I was also able to come full circle on the grief of the experience. During one of the regressions, a lot of emotion that was not present time came out of me. That experience remains one of the most potent expansive experiences I have ever had in my life. I not only processed present-time grief, I also processed past-time grief. This allowed me to resolve karma and connection/resonance to this situation or any that were similar. For this reason, I am a huge supporter of past-life regression. Whether or not you believe past lives exist, it is an amazing tool for clearing energy and expanding self-awareness.

Although I was immediately drawn to my boyfriend, I only spent a year with him rather than a lifetime. I learned enough from the previous incarnation and carried it forward to know I did not want to go down that road again, no matter how much I cared for him. This is an example of how the past can influence the now. Although everything is happening *now*, the past does create the present. Until the past is complete, it continues to create itself in our now and in our future experiences.

The following story provides a way to consider future in present time. I had a client whose parent was a Holocaust survivor. He carried forward anger, pain, and distrust from that experience. He was never able to separate from that experience to learn to be joyful. Consequently, he raised his children with an iron hand. He was truly a tyrant. He literally terrorized and bullied his kids. As they became adults, none of them wanted to be with him. They were completely uninterested. When they came of age, they couldn't wait to get away from him. The father was unable to see the connection of how being a bully and tyrant created a situation where his children did not want to be with him. All he could see was the pain of his own experience. He felt justified in everything he did. He was unwilling and unable to see any connection between his treatment of his kids in the past and how it influenced his present moment, and ultimately his future. His explanation for his adult children's behavior is that they were stupid, useless, awful kids.

A person with this identification is completely stuck on the pattern they are in. They refuse to consider any other possibility for a lot of reasons. They shift responsibility on to others for why they are unloved or unhappy. This represents an example of how that fixation looks in the continuum of past, present, future, and the eternal now.

The eternal now is the center of the universe, where divine intelligence exists. It is where enlightened entities live at all times. It is where each of us are striving to get to. Enlightened beings like Jesus, Buddha, and Swami Kriynanda reside here. The average person like me or you may be inching our way toward that ultimate reality. We are not there yet. Those enlightened masters lived the eternal now even in human form. Yet, through right thinking, meditation, personal responsibility, and joy, we all keep inching toward the center that is the eternal now. Every step we take toward that center, by cultivating an expanded awareness, moves us closer to that awakened and enlightened state.

When the soul takes a body, we choose a family a personality, and align with those people who will help us realize our spiritual goals. When we take a body, we activate our ego. To the degree we identify with life through the lens of the ego will determine the extent of our joy or lack of joy. The graphic on page 108 helps illustrate how we move ourselves closer to the infinite truth or how we keep ourselves away from truth and happiness. It is where and what we choose to put our attention upon that will determine our ability to feel joy.

Notice the now center in the circle of the graphic and notice all external experiences that revolve around the now. They represent moments in time when we exist in the human body. When we choose to take a human body, we automatically slip into the egoic perspective and begin to identify with physical experiences as the ultimate truth. It's the dance of duality in life. We have to survive physically, yet still understand that the physical experience is the ultimate illusion while ultimate truth resides in non-physical experience. To the degree we hold egoic identifications is to the degree we will remain in either a contracted or expanded position. The ego is concerned with avoiding discomfort. The soul is content with all experiences. Life simply is. Experience is a teacher, a mechanism for growth. Once the value of the experience has expired, our ability to cease identification with the experience causes us to evolve spiritually and energetically. Each time we progress beyond an experience, we inch closer and closer to the center of the eternal now and bliss.

The father of a dear friend, although very intelligent, spent all his time waiting for moments in which he could relive instances when he felt superior or in the "right" about something. No matter how much time passed between an event and the present moment, if he could find a way to bring up a situation from the past, and talk about how right he had been in that situation, he would do it. He loved to do that. His entire existence and validation to himself revolved around being right.

One day I asked him if he ever wanted to learn and grow from his experiences and understand what they all meant. As quickly as I got the words out, he barked back emphatically, "NO!" His identification, his value, and his perception of life was at its best reliving those moments when he was right. He didn't ever want to relinquish those stories or stop telling them over and over. Why would he? These memories were his source of happiness. He knew no other way to find happiness and did not want to learn another way at this point. The idea was far too threatening to the world he had created for himself. From his perspective, his reality, his happiness is what he has. He doesn't long for anything different.

The following graphic illustrates how we can fixate upon a point in time. To the degree we fixate on the point is how it becomes our reality.

When we are fixed on an idea, we don't see around the speck we are focused on. Our attention, just like my friend's father, was to stay right on the target, the dot. It was to hold on to that one place in time in which he found a moment of satisfaction.

Imagine you are holding a dark object close in front of your eyes. All you can see is dark. You would swear to everyone around you the world is dark. Life is dark. Dark is all there is. We would assert that perspective staunchly. As soon as we move the dark object away from our eyes, and give it a little space, our perspective changes. We become aware there is much more going on than what we originally considered. The ability to expand our perspective to see as many angles as we possibly can is the answer to enlightenment. That is the process of developing an expanded consciousness. Every step we take in expansion brings us closer to enlightenment and the eternal now, voiding discomfort. The soul is content with all experiences. They are all neutral.

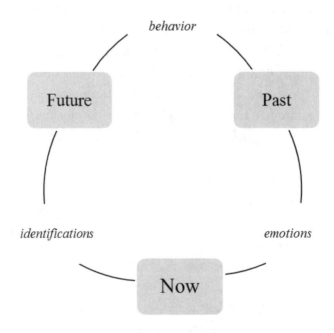

CHAPTER 7

Trust: How the Tangible Creates Itself

*"The best way to find out if you can trust
somebody is to trust them."*

—ERNEST HEMINGWAY

About five years ago, during the worst part of the recession when the real estate market was tanking, my income tripled. I began to speak to groups about prosperity and teach classes on cultivating abundance. This continues to be a cornerstone of much of my work because so many people need to understand it more fully. Of course the big question is always "How did you do it?" After I explain the tactics and strategies I used, which are practices available to anyone, I tell audiences that the number-one thing I did to create more money was to let go of my anger.

This is where things get fun and interesting. When I tell people that letting go of anger increased my income, they really scratch their heads. Kind of like a dog that cocks its head sideways. I began to break it down to the simplest possible level to ensure people understand how everything is connected, especially in our own personal universe and how that relates to income.

First, I have always been a hard worker. I came from an achievement-based family background. During much of my young life, I defined my value by how much I could do, how good my grades were, and what people thought of me. I shed that belief as I discovered that value is inherent, and nothing ever changes my value. I determine my value internally. That's when my income really shifted. I finally understood that working hard doesn't make me a better person. It's the content of my contributions that cause me to feel my value. That awareness allowed me to shed the "achievement" model and exchange it for an "allowing" model.

The achievement model says "I make it happen," "I go get it," and that means I am qualified, good, and smart. Achievement-based thinking suggests that outside accomplishments or stimulations will somehow make us feel successful, secure, or proud.

The allowing model says I honor the divine truth in me, and I allow it to emerge. As I allow my divine truth to emerge, my innate value becomes ever more present. As I honor my innate value, I allow abundance to realize itself in my life.

As I shed the achievement model, I still maintained a good work ethic and time management skills. As a working mother, I had to have these skill sets. The awareness of inherent value led me to live a purpose-driven life making a living at something I love to do. In the following statement are three elements of why I was able to triple my income in a down market.

1. I have a good work ethic. I am committed. I don't give up. I always look for new solutions if the idea I am using doesn't bring the result I want. I go back to the drawing board. I ask myself, "What do I have to give that I'm not giving?"

2. I am doing something I love. It is not work to get up to do my job. It is my life. I love it. I feel I have a purpose. I contribute to the well-being of others and life. It gives my life meaning.

3. I answer to myself. I measure myself only to myself. I may listen to the counsel of a wise friend or confidant, but *my* opinion is the one I honor. I know that no one but me knows my value or what I am capable of doing or being. I honor my divine essence and knowing.

Having these three elements in place put me far ahead of the game for the average person. I'm not afraid of hard work. I do what I love. I honor myself.

With these three pieces in place, the process became fine tuning. I approach creation from every aspect we know of in the human experience. I balance the mental, emotional, physical, and spiritual. Before I tripled my income, I was somewhat frustrated with my outcomes. I was doing okay, but didn't really have enough to enjoy any lifestyle. It was difficult to take a vacation or really save any money, or buy myself anything nice. I was paying my bills, barely, and some months I didn't know if I would make it. Month after month, I became exhausted with the worry and stress of wondering if I would have enough. There was a short period of time I actually needed food stamps to help feed my kids.

A time came when I remember having a conversation with myself. I said, "Why are all my clients doing so well and I'm struggling?" My answer was, "Why don't you take your own advice and find out?" So I did. I looked at my situation, as I would a client. I broke down my questions and concerns and considered exactly what I would say to a client in the same predicament. (I encourage all my clients to do this for themselves.)

What I noticed is that I was running a lot of "not enough" inner dialogue. I was thinking a lot about whether or not I would make my bills each month, and I was stressing over it and really worrying about it. As soon as my rent was paid, I was worrying if I would make rent the next month. At the same time, I was going through a divorce. My ex-husband didn't always pay child support in a timely manner or in the full amount. If he decided not to pay one month or to pay less, it would completely devastate me financially. He would often surprise me at the last minute when there was a shortage. I had to scramble. That made me really nervous and stressed out.

I found myself continually being angry and focused on what a loser he was and how badly he had screwed up our lives. There is truth in that. He did screw up our lives. In the Energy Game, it really doesn't matter if it's true or not that someone wronged us. We have to look at how we co-created the experience. We have to look at what was in it for us, not just what it took from us, and how we can grow from the experience. We can revel in victimization. It will never take us any place we want to go. We can stay there as long as we like. We get what we get from digesting that energy. I chose my ex-husband. I chose to stay. I chose to participate in the dynamics that ultimately resulted in an unpleasant ending.

What matters is the energy we choose to consume and bathe in on a daily basis. I am certainly entitled to my anger. I have every right in the free world to be angry. No one would fault me for it. What was it getting me? I reflected on what I teach others. Anger is a contracted life-stunting frequency. I can consume it all I want. I can consume it all day long, seven days a week. Again, consuming it will never take me any place I want to go. Anger, a contracted vibration, was at the foundation of all my creations. How could I possibly allow abundance in using a contracted frequency? We tend to think that our money is in one place, our relationships are in another, and our careers are in another. They are all in the same place, created from the same frequencies. Sometimes we are naturally higher-functioning in one area more than another, but ultimately how we show up in one area is how we are showing up in other areas. There is a common thread that goes through our entire personal universe.

In a moment, I had clarity. I suddenly realized I was sabotaging my own expansion and prosperity by holding onto the anger. When I realized that holding on to anger was prohibiting my own abundance, I let it go. It was like suddenly realizing I had leeches all over my body. I started pulling them off one by one. I let go of seven years of anger toward my ex-husband. Anger for him not being there in the way I wanted him to be, anger for the future I saw for myself before our relationship ended, anger about his instability and lack of dependability, and anger at myself for abandoning myself in the relationship. I colluded in my own self-abandonment and allowed those diminishing relationship dynamics to take a toll on my heart. In a moment, I released it all. I was and felt free. I didn't know how at that time, but I did know my life would change because I felt different inside.

Timing is everything. Was it coincidence? I had been processing the ending of my marriage for a long time. I had also been listening to some NLP (neuro-linguistic programming) CDS by John Assaraf for abundance and well-being. As soon as I connected to my own self-sabotaging methods with clarity, I moved away from them immediately. I was sick and tired of feeling awful. Sometimes that's what it takes for any of us to move forward. We have to be so sick and tired of the status quo that we open ourselves to something new.

From that place of realization that I was sabotaging myself, I began to look more closely at my inner dialogue. I learned a method that stopped me from worrying about money. Just like anger, worry is a contracted vibration that will never take me anyplace I want to go. I developed a strategy of stopping myself when my mind was looping on worry and taking a few moments to reject it. I would take the time to acknowledge that I always paid my rent on time and had never missed a payment. Life was indeed supporting me. I honored that. I began to consciously feel trust that I was being supported by life. I began to choose to replace worry with trust in all situations in my life. I trained myself to stay in the moment of contemplation until the worry stopped and trust took over. Every time I stopped the worry loop, I was always grateful. Every single time, within a couple of days of whatever caused the concern, it solved itself effortlessly. I was so happy that I didn't waste two, three, or four days worrying needlessly. I preserved and honored my life force energy. I didn't squander it on contracted frequencies that self-sabotaged.

As I released the anger and began to reject worry as a valid response to life, my creative energy and space began to expand. Suddenly I had ideas about projects I had never considered. I began to have a new confidence for life that I didn't before. Suddenly my space that had previously been occupied by anger and worry was now free to create and bring in new prosperity. I was having fun immersed in my creativity. I had been full of contracted vibrations. I had to empty out those vibrations to make room for new vibrations.

I created two new programs, plus several workshops that were new to my business. I wrote a new book. I created a DVD entitled *Making the Connection to Your Abundance*. I joined a new radio network with a broader reach than I had before. I booked speaking engagements at new higher-profile venues than I had ever appeared at before. All the while I was loving every step of creating products and sharing my message and information in new ways. It didn't feel like work; it felt like I was doing my life's work. People could not consume my programs or my products fast enough. I was connecting with people in a new way because I was approaching my life and my work with a new level of love and abundance in my own energy.

I educate myself on marketing principles and do what I can to put my best foot forward at all times. It all really is an Energy Game. If I had not released the anger or trained myself to reject worry as a valid response, I would not have had the room in my awareness or my life to create new programs. I would not have had the confidence or energy to put my message out in new ways to be received. I correlate the release of anger and worry directly with my ability to create and bring in new money. Without that shift, I would have remained stuck in lower-level frequencies experiencing results that lower-level frequencies provide.

Yes, I employ marketing strategies that are available to everyone. I work hard. I also make sure I have space in my life. Space is equally as important as action. With an equal balance of space and activity, I can maintain balance in all areas of my life. I make sure to get exercise to keep my body content and healthy. I eat foods that support feeling well. I make time for my relationships, my family, and my friends. One area of abundance is not more important than another area. I want to have it all. I think having it all is available to everyone.

When I am teaching people how to double or triple their income, it isn't just about marketing or hard work. It is about helping them identify energies they consume and to observe the content of their internal dialogue. When the internal dialogue is peaceful, abundant, confident, and happy, the outcomes will reflect that. People will consciously or unconsciously experience those frequencies and want to have them in their own life. Expansion to double or triple your income requires that you think out of the box. You have to go outside of what you have been doing to bring something new in.

Mostly what I share with my clients as I explain the Energy Game is that the creative process is an exchange process and a collaboration. As we resonate frequencies into consciousness, consciousness responds perfectly to us. The more expansive the frequencies in our personal universe, the more expansion we are able to receive from consciousness. An expanded consciousness is required to receive abundance. These are high-level frequencies. If we are not expanded, there is no room for "big" anything to come into our experience. We have to create the space first, and then the universe responds accordingly.

Trust is the primary element in this exchange. We develop trust with the divine as we would any other relationship: step by step and over time. When clients are first beginning this relationship of trust, I give them small goals. If someone wants to double their income, I will start the process by asking them to increase it by 5 percent. Most people don't really believe they can double or triple their income, or they are thinking too much inside of the box to recognize opportunities.

We have to silence the ego mind to allow them to go after something they believe they can accomplish. After they apply the principles to expand 5 percent, the person feels confident. "Yes, I can do this; I understand." Then they set a new goal. As the confidence and trust with the exchange process deepens, it begins to have a snowball effect. The person builds momentum and success happens. When one becomes adept at the exchange and trust process, it adds a new dimension and reliability to their creative process.

There are common impediments people experience in expansion. One is what I refer to as a "set point." Many of us have financial set points just as we have temperature set points in our body or weight set points. If we have been making $50,000 for 15 years, and we begin a process of trying to double or triple that income, we often have to adjust the financial set point as well. We have been conditioned over time to acknowledge that number as our top number. I use a variety of visualization tools that help clients actively move their set point.

One of the easiest tools is to imagine in your mind is a thermometer. The numbers, rather than temperature, are salary numbers. At the bottom is your current number. At the top of the thermometer is the number you want to reach. In your mind's eye, you watch the mercury rise to see if the mercury will rise to the number you are trying to reach. About 90 percent of the time, people cannot get the mercury to rise all the way to the top to their number. Or it will rise and fall. They can't maintain it. Then we have to go back in and start to deconstruct any limited thinking around abundance and extinguish any ideas of lack that the person may be holding. After that, we go back to try the thermometer visualization again. When we do this two or three times, most people are able to get their mercury to rise to the number.

This illustrates how our conditioning influences our ability to expand. We have to be proactive and engaged with our process to effect change. Too often, people want a spontaneous result. It isn't that spontaneous changes can't occur. "Spontaneous" is not the most common or reliable method. We have to actively move our energy around to affect a different outcome. If we do so with consistency, we will absolutely create new rhythms and new momentums that lead us to our goals and dreams.

Trust: How the Tangible Creates Itself

On my radio show, I have had a number of people call in suffering from long-term unemployment and chronic financial problems. These two callers represent those situations well.

Mark from Cleveland began calling the show. He was a family man, used to being employed most of his adult life. His children were now in their teens. He was having difficulty finding work of any type. Even though he had a lot of experience, he wasn't even able to find a commission sales job.

I began to delve into his situation, and the first thing that became apparent is that he was depressed, for more reasons than being unemployed. We all tend to feel that life is a linear experience to a certain degree. We can simply line up the events we want to occur and put dates by them. For example, when we arrive at certain dates and our outcome hasn't arrived, or circumstances haven't changed, we become lost about how to regroup and restart our life. Mark was the perfect example of this.

One of his daughters was now 19 years old. She was a talented and creative young woman with aspirations to become a model and an actress. Her dreams were coming true. She had recently left home to go to New York for modeling work. This left a hole in the family, as she was the consummate good girl, good student who did everything right. On the other side, Mark had a son who was a good person, but who was struggling in his life. He still had several years before he graduated high school. Mark and his wife were left with a difficult child while coping with the loss of the person who always brought levity and ease to their situation. There was a level of grieving and frustration that neither Mark nor his wife knew what to do with. Most of us feel it's wrong to be upset with our child or feel disappointed. Parents don't feel they have the right to have any feeling other than pride for their kids. Mark was not in touch with all these dynamics and how they were weighing on him energetically.

Many of us begin our young lives thinking we will go to college, start a career, get married, have a couple kids, and then our life is set. Not enough people plan for the chapters of their life after the kids leave home, or when children require extra attention to get them to age 18 and become self-sufficient. In the same conversation, it is now typical for people to change jobs six or seven times or more in a lifetime.

Mark was not prepared to cope with the changing business world or the technological skills that are now required in the marketplace. He felt a level of incompetency in his ability to put himself out into the world. He found himself applying for lesser and lesser roles to get "something." He was sending himself a message that he was incapable and no longer valid in life. Couple this message with the grief in his family dynamic, and that energy combination is about as dense and sad as it gets. There is loss, change, frustration, and an overall feeling of being overwhelmed, outmanned, and under-gunned. Energetically, this is a recipe for stagnation. Nothing can happen in this energy.

Men, even more than women, tend to want to live in their heads, be "the analyzer," and try to make everything practical. This is a wonderful skill set. Yet, the skill set we all need to know is how to evolve ourselves in our own lives when we hit a wall. This requires an ability to be able to listen to our hearts and move away from "make-it-happen" energy. With Mark and many people, we have to allow the sorrows of our life experience room to breathe. Most of us are afraid of our sorrows and refuse to be with them. Sorrow offers an enormous opportunity to expand ourselves. When we aren't in sorrow, we have no motivation to shift, change, or learn anything new. When we are in sorrow, the way out of it is to expand into our greatness by learning more about ourselves. Sorrow is a golden opportunity to emerge into more of who we are by developing different aspects of ourselves that are dormant or undiscovered. This is how we learn and grow on the planet. When we are comfortable, we don't grow.

With Mark, I had to teach him to give himself permission to own his disappointment, his fear, and his self-doubt. After that point, he was able to see that a whole new world was waiting for him. Mark made a typical mistake that a lot of people make: he lumped all of his feelings and thoughts into one situation. Rather than become awake to his grief about changes in his life, his fear about his abilities, or his frustration, he focused all his attention on "I can't get a job and I don't have enough money." If we are not awake and responsive to our internal world, it doesn't deactivate its influence on our creative process. All those frequencies and emotions are still working to create our experience.

I remember a caller, Jesse, from Los Angeles, who had a similar problem to Mark. When he called the show, he had been unemployed for about eight months. I could tell he was discouraged and afraid, and everything felt extremely serious in his energy. I encouraged him to stop his job search temporarily, and go to the beach and relax. I wanted him to have a good time and change how he was feeling in his life. The beach was some place he really loved. Essentially, I wanted him to insert fun energy into his space to create an opportunity for something new to come in. He was completely contracted. Just like the fist closed tightly, if you squeeze hard enough nothing can get in or out. Our energy field is the same. When we are contracted nothing gets in or out. Given that Jesse had nothing to do anyhow, as he wasn't employed, he decided to take my advice. He had nothing to lose.

After four days of being at the beach, he returned home to find a message waiting for him on his answering device. It was an employer who had his resume from over six months ago. They had kept his on file as someone they would be interested in when an opening arose. Was it timing? What is coincidence? I would say yes to both except I have watched the phenomenon for more than 30 years. Time and time again, I have seen that when we shift internally, our external world shifts. We hold the key. Perhaps in Jesse's situation, the energy was accumulating and waiting to come in. He had to let it in. Once he relaxed and inserted fun frequencies into his world, his circumstance changed. He allowed his divine opportunity to emerge.

Quantum physics has demonstrated time and again that what we think about something modifies it. Further, that thought precedes matter. Everything is connected. Those things we call "coincidence" are more demonstrations of energy aligning perfectly based upon intention and divine collaboration. When we become intentional with this process and learn to stay awake in our personal universe, we really can play the Energy Game and influence our outcomes in amazing and powerful ways. There is nothing we cannot create if we are willing partners in our own creative process. It is when we deny and resist our realities that we begin to feel life is random and that we have no power to effect change in our outcomes. As with both Mark and Jesse, learning to insert high-level frequencies when we feel contracted is a very valuable practice that works.

In Mark's case, he was lumping all his feelings together, which caused him to be overwhelmed. When he was able to separate his feelings and address them one at a time, he finally connected with employment. He made space. Before that he was like a tangled ball of yarn. There was no rhyme or reason to his reality. With Jesse, he was so contracted he was impeding any opportunity from entering his realm. As soon as he inserted high-level frequencies into his experience and "created space," the phone rang.

When we play the Energy Game, when we trust, and when we practice collaboration and intentional exchange with consciousness, we will see the results. We will have success, and we can build on the relationship we now have with the divine in more potent and profound ways.

— CHAPTER 8 —

Karma

"Like gravity, karma is so basic we often don't even notice it."
—SAKYONG MIPHAM

The idea of cause and effect is accessible to most people in some form. Modern culture provides a measure of this through the penal system. We know that if we perform some type of negative behavior, there will be some type of negative repercussion. For the most part, we understand there are consequences to our choices. Most of us don't have a solid grasp on what karma is or how we can recognize it in life. We don't understand that the many layers and dimensions of who we are affect our creative process. That's where we need to begin to understand our relationship to karma.

We are always in a creative process. We create with our intention. We create with our emotions. We create with our intellect. We create from what we don't know as well. We can call that the unconscious, that part of us that doesn't know what we don't know. Some of that may be karma. Some of it may be unrealized self-potential. There are ways to navigate these layers if we take the time to be with ourselves and listen to our process. We can navigate them step by step, mostly by learning to pay attention to how we feel to understand it in the totality of our experience.

Most of us don't know what to do about karma, or if we should do anything about it at all. There is also a lot of misunderstanding about the word and idea of karma. Most often I hear people use statements like "I have good karma" or "I have bad karma." Karma is neither good nor bad. Karma is a word that describes in totality the accumulated effect of all the decisions we have made in this lifetime and past lifetimes. Karma is our unlearned lessons. It always presents itself in some way. An easy way to think of karma is that it is glue that connects everything that is. Karma connects us to everything we have done, everything we are doing, and everything we will do. When karma of lower frequencies has been resolved, then we no longer contend with those frequencies. We do not resonate them into consciousness any longer. We will not receive any more experiences from the karma.

We have energy centers throughout our bodies called chakras. These centers house all the information from all of our experiences, past and present. Let's say you are in your 50s. When you were in your 20s you had a negative experience with a lover. You elected to simply leave the lover behind you. The interaction was too taxing, and you felt it was just best to move on. You got a sense of relief that you no longer had to deal with that person. You feel it was done and over because you didn't have to be with them any longer. The experience of "negative" is still registered in your energy centers. At some point in the continuum of your life, now or in the future, in order to reach enlightenment, you will have to come to balance with those frequencies. They will come up again at some point and in some form in order for you to resolve them at a higher level. This is what we do energetically. Step by step, we simply take our energy up one notch at a time and get ourselves to the next highest vibration we can hold.

Imagine if the schism occurred in another lifetime. You may not have memory when you meet that person again. You will be drawn to them or repelled by them for some unknown reason. Your energy centers have memory. On our path to enlightenment, it can only occur as we balance all the frequencies in our energy centers and bring them to higher frequencies. Even if you choose not to deal with the past lover from 30 years ago in this lifetime, you will have to deal with them at some point until you find a way to reach harmony in your own system. What the other person does in relationship to you is their karma. What you do in relation to the other person is your karma. How you feel. How you resolve it internally. How free you are is the test of resolved or unresolved karma.

There are three primary questions in life that we all need to answer. If we use these questions to measure our feelings, we will come upon an answer that will take us to higher frequencies. When we come upon struggles or forks in the road, or need an answer to a question, or if we simply answer these three questions to ourselves, we will be able to determine the answer that is in our highest and best interest. These questions are:

1. Who am I?

2. What is lasting and real?

3. Where does my happiness come from?

When we ask ourselves who we are, we are forced to remember that we are spiritual beings. Then we follow the next conclusions. I am an honest, loving person with intention to do good in life. I choose to be a force for love on the planet.

When we ask what is lasting and real, we are forced to remember that life is on a continuum. If we want a benevolent outcome, we must sow the seeds of benevolence on our path. We can create our experiences from joy or from misery.

When we ask ourselves where our happiness comes from, we are forced to remember that is always an inside job. No one can give us happiness. It is our task to resolve our internal struggle that takes us away from happiness.

Whenever a question arises, if we measure it against these three questions, we will know which direction to go. It will become clear what course will cause us to expand.

Recently I was giving a presentation on abundance at a local metaphysical center. When it came time for the question-and-answer period, a man in the audience rose to ask a question about revenge and whether the ends justify the means. He had recently gone through a divorce and was quite unhappy about the amount of financial support he was required to pay his ex-wife. His question centered on his divorce and a large payout he had to give to his former wife. He wanted to know if he could do something "tricky" or get around the judgment so he could keep the money for himself. The idea of getting the upper hand felt very good to him. He wondered how that related to karma.

I asked him to formulate his question in the context of the three questions we must always ask ourselves.

1. Who am I?

2. What is lasting and real?

3. Where does my happiness come from?

Who am I, the man to the question? He is more than an ex-husband. He has greater purpose than to have or give money. His purpose was actually as a creative and engineer. When we go back to the identification of who we truly are, we become less interested in "winning" certain moments in life. They take on a different meaning.

What is lasting and real? What is lasting and real is true benevolence. When we cultivate benevolence and love in our lives, we always find more love and benevolence. If we cultivate resistance and anger, we will find more of that in our experiences. The audience member had to choose what he wanted to align with as real.

Finally, **where does my happiness come from?** Our happiness comes from internal balance and peace. No amount of money will ever make him feel better. If he seeks revenge, he will receive a momentary stimulation or satisfaction. It will actually reduce his life force energy, and his ability to "have" in live. It is an anti-abundance frequency. It will not replace his feelings of failure for his lost relationship or the frustration he has for finding himself in this predicament.

In these situations, the best we can do is to move ourselves bit by bit in the direction of expansion. Expansion rarely happens in large strides. It is our ongoing determination to move inch by inch in the present moment toward expansion that creates our shifts and permanent changes.

A couple weeks ago, my daughter, who is involved with Girl Scouts, had an event with them. It had been planned for a while. (It was now December, and the event was planned in September.) Three days before the event was to occur, I got word of the local tree lighting ceremony in my city. The date of the tree lighting had changed from a Saturday to a Friday. It was going to be the same evening as the Girl Scout event. This is an event I do with my family every year, and we enjoy it tremendously.

I emailed the Girl Scout leader and let her know what had happened. The event my daughter was to be involved in was a very casual happening. It was a movie night for new incoming Girl Scouts. I apologized for the late cancellation and, out of respect, asked her if my daughter could be excused. I fully expected it would be no problem. As it turned out, the Girl Scout leader was irritated, and she sent me an email that was a bit snarky. My immediate reaction was one of anger and irritation right back at her. The tree lighting ceremony is very important to our family. I knew everyone would be disappointed if we didn't go or we didn't take my daughter with us. Rather than respond, I sat with the emotions until the next day. I wanted to decide how best to handle it.

I talked to my daughter about the potential that she may not get to go. I felt I was in between a rock and a hard place. I wanted to teach my daughter responsibility and accountability, but the tree lighting is an annual family event. Rather than react inside with all the emotion I was feeling, I chose to allow more space into the situation. I took no action. Within a short period of time, I began to see that I was imposing the feelings of being in between a rock and a hard place upon myself. I had complete authority to take my daughter wherever I wanted to take her. In my heart, I also wanted the Girl Scout leader to support us. I wanted her permission. I didn't want her to be mad at us.

To get to my answer, my first step was to recognize that I already had the power to do what I wanted. I didn't need anyone's permission. That inched me closer to expansion. Then, I realized that although Girl Scouts is not a big deal to me, the Girl Scout leader eats, lives, and breathes Girl Scout activities. Every activity is a big deal to her and her family. I needed to have a broader understanding of her feelings. Once I did, I felt more compassion toward her and understood why she might be irritated. It caused me to relax inside. I again inched closer to an expanded awareness.

Finally, I reached back out to the Girl Scout leader and apologized for the last-minute cancelation and promised we would never do it again. When she responded, she was somewhat curt again, although less this time. She finished her email with "Have a good time." She got what she needed, which was to vent her frustration and disappointment. She also understood that I wanted her permission. She gave it. I got what I wanted and did so through an expanded act. I could have just said, "Go to hell. I'll do what I want." That doesn't feel good. Those are not abundant or expansive frequencies. The time I took to sort through everything made all the difference in the outcome.

The moral of the story is that expansion is something that happens inch by inch, in each moment. In each moment, we simply need to do the best we can to aspire to ideas, thoughts, and feelings that will take us to an expanded vision. Ultimately, it worked out for me and for the Girl Scout leader. We did not create any karma moving forward. The energy field was clear. We don't get out of karma by doing it badly. We get out of it through the willingness to say "I don't have to like this, but I will do the best I can to create a positive outcome."

In terms of energy, I have written briefly about our energy centers, chakras. In the chakras, we have what are called *vrittis*. There are many definitions to this word. For purposes of this offering, I will share the definition which provides information about how our system works to resolve karma.

I have already talked about how we inch our way along into expansion. I want to add in now the idea of vritti. Vritti, meaning "whirlpool," is a technical term in yoga. It is meant to indicate the contents of mental awareness that are disturbances in the medium of consciousness. In our chakras, it looks like a whirlpool, and acts like one. In the center of a whirlpool is the "eye." The eye represents the issue or the problem we have encountered. The energy swirling around it picks up speed and intensifies our original wound, so long as it remains intact.

When we are able to inch our way toward expansion in every thought and every choice, we reduce the charge on our vritti. We bring our chakras into balance on the specific frequency that has been activated.

When we are addressing karma in our life, we typically want to reduce it to "I don't have enough money" or "It's bigger than me." We throw up our hands, concluding that we don't have the capability to master our circumstance. That is absolutely untrue. In the case of money, you may or may not have a karma that indicates you will be rich in this lifetime. You can affect the quality of your experience in the lifetime, regardless of your karma.

The game of attraction is really about magnetism or resonance. As we raise our frequencies, our magnetism also raises. It changes how we resonate into consciousness. The level at which we resonate is how we attract prosperity in any form. So long as we inch our way in the direction of expanded consciousness, everything will fall into place. It is our resistance to what is, and our attachment to our expectation of what we should have, that causes us suffering.

Finally, I want to address the idea of intention. The divine is a benevolent consciousness. It knows our intention even before we make mistakes or poor choices. It knows our heart. Intention makes a difference in the type of karma we create for ourselves. For instance, if a person driving a car loses control and accidentally hits someone and kills him, the karma on this situation is significantly less potent than a driver who maliciously targets an individual and runs them down on the side of the road. The content of our intention matters. It may not erase the karma entirely, but it mitigates the potency. What we intend makes a difference. If you have a clear heart and a clear consciousness, and your desire and intention is to be a force for light, you will create less karma for yourself.

Karma, again, is simply the word that describes the accumulated effect of all our experiences. The more expansive we can become in our view, the more we will be able to recognize karma working in our life. Events that may seem random on the surface have an origin to them. We may not be able to understand in the present moment why something is occurring. There is a reason.

The good news is that it doesn't matter if an event happened 500 years ago or five hours ago. If we pay attention to how we feel, and seek to put ourselves into balance (meaning we feel at peace with our lives, our choices, and our present moment), we will clear out karma. We will equalize the frequencies and raise them.

One of my favorite exercises for changing our karma and reality is inserting high-vibration frequencies. It's a mini vacation. This insertion of high-vibration frequencies can have an enormous impact on your energy and your karma.

Another technique I love to share with clients is that of balancing chakras. There are varied approaches taught about this. My technique is to go into the chakra to see what is going on, and together we change what is happening in that energy center.

There are many different techniques and vehicles available to us to clear and align our energy centers. One is not better than the other. What matters is if you are ready to receive the benefit of moving energy in your space. All that is required is a desire to receive.

There are many practitioners, healers, and new age thinkers who have an arsenal of tools to help people clear their fields. All we have to do is ask for the right and perfect person to show up and they will. We are not resigned to karma that dictates our happiness and well-being.

CHAPTER 9

Marriage

"A good husband makes a good wife."
—John Florio

M arriage is a wonderful topic to explore. In addition to Western ideas of love and romance, the historical origins of marriage are quite interesting. It says a lot about why we are where we are today in modern times. There are many aspects and reasons marriage came to be. There are many influences from many parts of the world. Most of us don't consider historical perspectives when we talk about marriage.

One part of my job is talking to people about their relationship goals and needs. I talk to many women who are eager or desperate to be married. Yet, when I ask people why they want to get married, the answers are typically vague or short sighted. More often than not, it seems people marry because they believe they should. It is the right thing to do right now.

I have come to counsel most of my clients who are considering marriage to focus much more on the building blocks of creating a good marriage rather than planning a beautiful and expensive wedding. Most women devote all their attention to becoming engaged and then getting married. There is no plan for what will happen after the "I do's" have been said.

Marriage, in some form, has been around for as long as history has been recorded. Most often it was a mechanism used to bond families together. If powerful families bonded together they would amplify the family's power and influence, including being able to change laws or influence policy in their culture. In many cultures around the globe, regardless of socio-economic conditions, marriage was primarily a business arrangement.

In other cultures, marriage has been the mechanism to sanction sexual interaction or to begin the process of procreation. We take for granted a history of polygamy that exists around the globe. There has also been a monogamy-lite form of marriage that existed in the 19th century. Men could openly step out and be with other women. Women, of course, could not, but promiscuity for men was sanctioned legally. Eventually the Catholic Church defined monogamy as a standard. In the United States, marital rape was legal in some states until the 1970s. Women couldn't even open credit cards in their own name. Gender power and position have been a factor in marital arrangements and benefits. And up until the 1970s in some states, during a divorce, women would be entitled to spousal support but would have no power over community property issues. (For more information go to *www.professorshouse.com/Relationships/Marriage -Advice/Articles/Arranged-Marriage-Facts/#sthash.kJNRlByG.dpuf*)

I bring up these various perspectives on marriage because they all influence our beliefs and habits around marriage today. It has only been in the last 250 years that the notion of marriage for love has become popular, especially in the west. Polygamy is still practiced in some parts of the world. According to *www.poligamy.org*, polygamy is still a legal culture in more than 150 countries, including Africa, the Middle East, and most countries in the third world. Nigeria alone is home to more than 40 million polygamists. Arranged marriages are an accepted practice in Iran,

Iraq, Afghanistan, Japan, India, Bangladesh, and some Muslim countries. Arranged marriages also exist in China and Indonesia, and in cultures where Buddhism, Islam, and Hinduism are the predominant religions.

As we evolve on the planet and seek to elevate ourselves spiritually, both individually and collectively, all our relationships and how we manage them are in flux. Excluding reincarnation and the programming we bring with us in our chakras, there is a lot of confusion about what marriage is, what it is supposed to give us, and why we do it.

This story about Andrea's situations offers a typical perspective many women have when it comes to marriage. Andrea came to me for several sessions to talk about her life and her relationship with her on-again, off-again boyfriend John. As we spoke about her life circumstances, she had a lot of frustration and sadness about what she perceived to be his ability to commit. They had been in a long-distance relationship for almost five years. Although they had talked about moving in together and moving closer together, it never happened. At one point in the session, Andrea said "I just want the ring. I want to be engaged." I asked her why. No matter how hard I tried to get an answer from her, or how hard she tried to come up with an answer, she simply didn't' have one. It was just "I want the ring." There was a fantasy that somehow everything would come together perfectly if she just had the ring. "It will give me security." I tried to help Andrea see that a ring or any "thing" cannot provide security. It's merely a representation of an understanding two people share. She actually got a bit frustrated with me as I kept turning her attention in the direction of answering the question.

Andrea wanted to idealize the answer to her issues with John. It was easier than getting real with herself about her flailing relationship with him. She wanted me to jump on board with the idea and say "Yes, a ring will really do it for you." She was glossing over the reality that they couldn't even get in the same town after five years of dating. She was unwilling to look at many aspects of their relationship that were frustrating and unfulfilling.

I think Andrea's scenario is similar to what a lot of people struggle with. They have been taught erroneous concepts about relationships and given mixed messages from culture, many of which have been formed by history. We are taught that we should be monogamous and be with one person. We are taught that marriage is the answer to loneliness, to a rich sex life, and to the man of our dreams. We are taught that one person will do it all for us. Yet, one of the chronic things I see in my practice is married couples who are lonely in their marriages. I see non-existent sex lives. I see people who married for love yet stay married for reasons other than love. We are shown by modern culture that the divorce rate, depending upon the source, is 40 to 50 percent. Despite the rules of marriage, people still break them. There is no security in an external structure designed to regulate behavior.

We know that marriage doesn't always work. Most of us have very little idea why marriage doesn't work. Between the conditioning of culture, the evolving nature of relationships in modern times, and our lack or maturity, we find ourselves focused on the elements that can't possibly bring us happiness. This does not even address the aspect of karma in individual situations.

Andrea and I agreed to disagree about the ring. I took a different approach with her. We moved into strategizing about what might need to occur for her and John to get in the same town or move in together. That felt much better to her. Together, we created a series of steps that she felt were very reasonable and sensible. I asked her to stay in touch with me regarding the steps. If John was not able to meet the steps, I wanted to know why and how she wanted to proceed from there. When she left my office, she was excited about sharing this information with John so that they could move their relationship forward.

I didn't hear from Andrea for a while. About four months later, she reached out to schedule a session. She indicated she and John had broken up. It simply wasn't going to work between them, and she was done. Just as she had done with the ring, she was unable to go deeply into her process to really understand why it didn't work with John.

As with our first meeting, we talked about relationships, how they are created, and the ring and its meaning. Afterward, she was a little closer to herself and truth, but she was still not quite ready to take the "fantasy" of the ring and the relationship out of her mind. In this session, she was focused on a new love interest. She felt that this new man was going to be her answer. She was convinced that John had been the problem. Now that she had found a more compatible partner, things should move along just fine. I congratulated her on her new relationship and sent her on her way.

Another few months passed and Andrea returned again. This time, she indicated she and John had been talking again. He tracked her down and had proposed to her. He wanted to come to the city and go ring shopping with her during the upcoming weekend. They still weren't in the same town, so she had mixed feelings about it. The ring and the proposal didn't have the same appeal it once did. The fantasy had been ruined for her. The cumulative effect of her long-term disappointment with John, coupled with an expanding awareness about what her needs were, left her somewhat flat about the proposal and the ring. Yet a part of her still recognized she had an opportunity to grab that thing she had wanted for so long. She came to me to sort it out. She was wondering now if she had made a mistake and needed to go back to John.

As we talked, she recognized that John was coming back into her experience not make her feel loved and appreciated but to hold on to her. He was also afraid of moving on after their five-year relationship. He didn't know who he was going to be without her. Ultimately, Andrea decided not to get the ring or to reconnect with John. She moved forward with the new relationship.

In the past two years since Andrea left her relationship with John, she has dated multiple men. Each time she begins, there is still a good dose of fantasy about the person and what they will give to her that clouds her judgment. As the relationships progress, she is once again met with disappointment.

Andrea's story continues today. She is evolving, growing, and changing at the pace she can. She is a lovely and bright woman, and I expect she will connect to love at some point. Love is so much about how we feel about ourselves, coupled with our beliefs about what a relationship is supposed to do for us. Therein lives another sabotaging influence of perfectly good relationships.

Men and women both come to relationships with a set of expectations about what the other is supposed to do for them. In committed relationships, it is not unreasonable to expect certain things from your partner. They are things that are mutually agreed upon, as the relationship develops. Too often men and women have unspoken expectations. "He should buy me expensive presents on holidays." "She should have sex with me every day, twice a day." "He needs to take care of me, financially, sexually, and emotionally." "She needs to cook meals, keep the house clean, and make sure my needs are taken care of."

Many of these expectations are taught to us through culture, family, and movies. We aren't even aware that they are operating in our decision-making and our life. These expectations create disappointment, anger, and resentment, which are all killers and suppressors of love. Our ability to identify our expectations before we begin acting upon them is crucial in any relationship, let alone marriage.

In addition to expectations, there is a natural rhythm that occurs in all romantic relationships.

1. Honeymoon/The Time of the Anesthetic

This describes the energy of the first few months of a new relationship. All we see and feel is the wonder of each other. We feel we have found our soulmate, and that our prayers have been answered. I also refer to this period as the time of the anesthetic. We likely encounter "red flags" or incompatibilities we have with a partner, but are so enamored and caught up in the new feelings, we ignore the information. We tell ourselves the "thing" that came up doesn't really matter. We don't address it. Or we downplay its importance.

A funny example is the old saying of two people newly in love. The woman tells a friend, "We are so in sync, we can finish each other's sentences." Two years down the road, the woman says to her partner "Will you will stop interrupting me?"

Even during the honeymoon, those things that are going to be core issues between couples always show up in some form. I've seen it for decades in my clients and in my own life. That issue that comes up right away is the issue you will be working on 10 years from now in your marriage, if you don't resolve it.

The honeymoon provides us a grace period in which we allow ourselves to get close to someone else and reactivate our belief in love and happy endings.

2. Bumping Up Against the Wounding

Somewhere between months three and four is where couples begin to bump up against each other's wounding. When I use the word *wounding*, I mean core issues, or those things an individual has not resolved in their emotional realm. The beauty of all this is that we come together to help each other heal. That's what we are really doing, in the name of love. Relationships are the best mechanisms for growth on the planet. We don't understand how relationships work or how to interact inside of them. We have received so much programming and misinformation from the past that most people do not know how to navigate the course or manage the feelings that arise when we begin to expose ourselves to another person.

It's true that we feel drawn to people who have the potential to help us heal our own wounding. That doesn't mean we aren't supposed to enjoy ourselves, or revel in love, sex, vacations, or anything else. Relationships are supposed to include enjoyment, companionship, and offer a sense of belonging. There is more to it.

When the wounding shows up, most people translate it in the language of a specific behavior. "Would you stop leaving the toothpaste cap off?" "You are always late, and that really pisses me off!" "You spend too much time with your friends." "You drink too much." Most of these statements are really cover stories for something that is being triggered inside of each of us. The most common culprits are:

1. **Lack of trust.** This really means "I don't trust myself to know if you are real."

2. **Low self-worth or lack of deserving.** This really means "I can't open up and stay open."

3. **Unresolved childhood trauma.** This really means "You keep doing it to me."

4. **Fear of intimacy.** This really means "No one is going to hurt or control me."

This is the critical time for most couples. A couple's ability to understand their own triggers, and to learn how to use language that expresses their process from an "I" position, is almost always the key. The closer we get to each other (the good stuff), the closer we also get to our wounding.

Most often couples point the finger at each other and insist that the other is doing something to cause their discomfort. This may be true at some point in some way. The ability to speak from a true heart-centered "I" position is the most potent and loving communication couples can have. Consider a statement such as "You are always late, and that is so inconsiderate." Rather than "My mom was always late to pick me up from school. It made me feel so afraid and unimportant. When you are late, I become afraid you aren't coming back. I get scared." That is something a person can understand. Otherwise all the other person hears is "I'm failing you." "I'm disappointing you." "I'm a bad person."

It's difficult, especially for men, to cope with the idea that they have failed their partner. In this reframing of a conversation, the woman addresses two things:

1. She was deeply wounded in childhood by her mother's behavior.

2. Her new partner's behavior is unintentionally activating the old wound.

There is only so much the other person can do to mitigate the impact of our wounding. Once we can speak open and honestly about it, we have to give it some attention, and actively engage in releasing and healing it. In the relationship scenario, the exposure of wounding shines a light on what the individual needs to work on. Her partner now has valuable information about his girlfriend. If he loves her and wants to be a good partner, he will recognize that his tardiness can be painful to her. He can choose to alter his behavior to make life more comfortable for her or not. This act encourages true intimacy. The wound served as an opportunity for the couple to get to know one another better and to become closer. If we allow the triggers to drive our communication, they will drive us apart.

If our partner doesn't alter their behavior, that's a dynamic and information that will help the other determine if that person is a good match for them. The point being made here is that each of us has to do our own personal work. We rush to get off of our own pain and project it on to our partner. We have an expectation that our partner needs to make it better for us. So long as we approach our relationships from this perspective, we are going have trouble sustaining intimate connection. We keep the focus outside of ourselves.

There's a movie I've seen many times on TV called *He's Just Not That Into You*. It has four romantic story situations going on throughout the movie. They are all facing life questions about love. One couple, played by Jennifer Connolly and Bradley Cooper, have been married a few years. They met in college. In the story, some distance has come between them and they have no sex life. They have normalized their "friend" marriage. Jennifer is focused on a home remodel and potentially becoming pregnant. Bradley has a brief affair with Scarlett Johansson. However, that isn't ultimately what breaks up the marriage. Jennifer's character is wounded around the fact that her father was a smoker and died of lung cancer. Bradley's character struggles with a cigarette addiction. Throughout the movie, she questions him about his cigarette smoking, and he insists he is not smoking. Even when he reveals his infidelity, rather than focus on that, Jennifer says "It was you who was smoking, wasn't it? What part of my 'father died of lung cancer' don't you get?" In the movie, Bradley hears her wounding. She is afraid the same thing will happen to him that happened to her father. She needs him to hear her. Bradley does not hear her or value her enough to honor that. That is a scenario in which one part of the couple has expressed their true fear, and the other doesn't respond as they are needed. Jennifer's character ends the marriage by leaving a note and a carton of cigarettes.

With the awareness that we come together to help each other heal, we can choose to help one another heal by being kind and supportive friends and lovers. This is the only path to find out if a partner is right for us. We have to be able to show who we truly are, wounding and all, to see how our chosen partner will respond to our unique set of energies and circumstances. Sometimes they will respond the way we want. Other times they will not. As with the previous movie example, Bradley was unable to address his cigarette addiction. There were other issues, of course. The lies began to pile up, creating distance between the couple, and ultimately lack of trust, or any feeling of safety. Once the relationship breaks down to that degree, no matter how much caring existed at one time, the two people can't be together anymore.

Most people unfortunately have little idea how to navigate an intimate relationship. When they begin to bump up against the wounding, rather than seeing the wounds as opportunities to heal and come closer, the interactions turn into power struggles. "Why won't you spend more time with me?" "Why won't you visit my family with me?" "You are always late!" "You are inconsiderate!" The conversations become about topics of contention rather than focusing on the issue that is driving the discomfort. "You left a glass out on the counter. I've told you 10 times I can't stand that. You are still doing it." "I'm tired of you nagging me." "You can't control me."

Couples go round and round, never getting to the true source of their pain. They can end relationships never even knowing why they ended. They simply point the finger at the other as the source of their pain. That doesn't mean that our partners may at some point unintentionally or intentionally injure us. That's different. In this common pattern, frustration and disappointment create a buffer between the love couples once felt and the hope they had for their life together. Interactions become about who is right and who is wrong, rather than "What do you need?" and "How can I help?" Couples pit themselves against one another rather than learn how to work together and come closer together.

3. Women are the Leaders in Relationships

This topic is another critical point in relationship dynamics that many people don't understand. It isn't exactly about gender, but it is. Women are physiologically different than men. Our brains are wired up differently. Women tend to communicate more effectively than men, focusing on how to create solutions by talking through issues and utilizing non-verbal cues such as tone, emotion, and empathy. Men tend to be more task-oriented and less talkative. Men have a more difficult time understanding emotions that are not explicitly verbalized, while women tend to intuit emotions and emotional cues. Men process better through the left brain, women through the right brain. The part of the brain that influences our ability to do math, the inferior parietal lobule, is much bigger in men than women. This doesn't mean women can't do math or excel in math. Men just have a larger mass area. In women, the larger right side of the other part of the brain helps them solve problems more creatively, and they are more aware of feelings while communicating. I share this for the physical reality that is different between the genders. We all know that women's bodies create life. That causes a very different set of frequencies, considerations, and perspectives. (All of this information and more can be found at *www.mastersofhealthcare.com /blog/2009/10-big-differences-between-mens-and-womens-brains/*)

Women do not lead in relationships by verbal cues. It isn't that women should not discuss or have conversations, but rather they must lead through behavior. When we lead with truth, compassion, and sincerity, if a man loves us he will follow our lead. In the previous example, when I referenced a fictional case in which the woman described her mother always being late, and how scared and insignificant that made her feel, that is an example of leading. Rather than telling our partner they have failed, we demonstrate what trust and honest communication looks like. Rather than attacking and making ourselves "right," we seek to understand rather than do battle to win. Doing battle to win is most often a protection and defense response. When a woman behaves how she wants to be treated, if a man loves her, he will follow suit. Men want to please women. We have to teach them how to do that. Men typically, not always, don't know how to do that with the same skill level a woman does or can, in part because of our physiological differences.

There are always exceptions. This is typical. These statements are for those people, men and women, who are honest and doing their best in life. We may encounter unscrupulous types. If you are grounded in integrity. you will spot them very quickly.

Marriage is similar but different to relationships and dating. When we are trying to create a marriage, we have to examine our motivations differently. While trying to create a relationship, we look into our beliefs and our creative mechanism differently, as described in a previous chapter.

Once in a committed relationship like marriage, the causes that make them successful are different. We have evolved from just being in a relationship to attempting to create a partnership that will last the lifetime. Within that context, there are many considerations, including karma.

In a marriage, we contend with religious preferences, parenting choices, division of labor, distribution and management of finances, extended family, and others goals we will make together as a partnership. Many times, couples do not consider these elements when deciding to partner. They don't consider what religion they will raise their children or why. They don't thoroughly talk through their financial considerations or their financial styles. They don't cover in-law issues or beliefs on parenting. They marry with the idea that love will conquer all and they will see eye to eye. As life creates itself, many times these differences tear couples apart.

In arranged marriages, often these types of considerations are known. The "love" factor is not part of the decision process. It's more about creating an alliance and situation that will be productive for the families. There are variations on the arranged marriage scenario. In relationship to Western culture's approach toward partnering, we could use a dose of practicality when we choose to marry.

The other factor comes in on the energetic level. We have and make agreements with various people before we incarnate on the planet. We have a purpose beyond our romantic objectives. For some people, being in a long-term relationship or marriage is part of their purpose. They will not fulfill the goals of their life if they are not in relationships. Some people have multiple mate agreements in the energy in the lifetime. If one long-term marriage dissolves, another will come in quickly in order for that person to remain in a marital situation.

When we have a mate agreement with someone for our lifetime it may also include soulmate agreements, task agreements, support agreements, and various other agreements that are unique to the situation. Again, they may have nothing to do with love, other than the underlying loving nature of the soul who wants to help the other on their path to enlightenment. Some or all of these ideas can and will play into whether or not we marry and stay married. Almost 100 percent of the time, from all I have seen energetically, we choose to be with people with whom we have shared experience before. That means we have karma to resolve. It can also mean we enjoy and trust another.

Historically, women had few rights and options, and little power. Marriage was absolutely necessary for an essence to have room to create or expand in the human experience. In modern times, as humanity evolves, women have more options. The souls that are coming to the planet now, and that have been coming to the planet for the last 50 years or so, have a more aggressive agenda than in previous cycles. Everything is accelerating for some purpose. My view is that the planet needs a strong feminine energy to help bring balance to the chaos that has been created on the planet.

In modern times, we are dealing with a collective consciousness around marriage. We are also dealing with our individual karmas with other people and our individual motivations to expand and fulfill our purpose(s). As we move forward in modern times, culture is being required to learn more about what makes relationships come together and stay together. We are also learning what pulls people apart. In the context of this spectrum, we are learning that all relationships are not meant to last the lifetime. Longevity does not necessarily equal quality. The model upon which marriage was based is now fluid and, in some forms, obsolete.

There are people who still come together and stay together for the lifetime. That's a wonderful thing. Often the purpose of those couples is united on deeper levels. They may have family agreements with task agreements, or other agreements beyond love that make the relationship last. What each soul intended to accomplish in the lifetime will also determine whether a long-term marital partner actually supports or reduces their opportunity to fulfill that purpose.

We are no longer in a place where women must rely upon men to support them financially. Women in particular are evolving at a significant pace. They are changing the energetic contributions to the world and the collective consciousness. A balance of feminine and masculine energies are required to heal the planet, sustain life, and create solutions to answer impending global challenges. How we partner, why we partner, who we partner with, and how we resolve karma all play a role in why marriages last and don't last. The day-to-day skill sets that are necessary to sustain marriages are very different than what they were just 50 years ago. It is my expectation that the definition of marriage and its purpose will continue to redefine itself as we learn to balance our respective strengths in the global picture of life.

We have a luxury on the planet of hundreds of religions. Only a handful dominate our awareness. But nonetheless, they can be vehicles to connect to spiritual truth. Most often, I observe that despite all these options to connect to spiritual truth, we are spiritually bankrupt. When we do not have adequate spiritual awareness, and we couple that with limited emotional flexibility, we will not be successful in our relationships. Although a few may defy that reality through will, skill, and karma, the collective truth remains constant. We will not thrive. Marriage is so much more than having a relationship. It encompasses the purpose of another individual. It involves resolution of karma. It requires a different commitment to life than simply being in a relationship. It is a way of life. In this age, women have many more choices available to them. They can opt not to marry, as can men. That does not have to be negative. Rather it is indicative of the evolution of our consciousness on the planet, and that we need all the energies of both genders to make sure we are creating a reality that supports a loving planet.

CHAPTER 10

Parenting

"A person soon learns how little he knows
when a child begins to ask questions."
—RICHARD L. EVANS

There are few topics that inspire potent feelings in the way parenting can. The only other topic that comes close in my mind is when Democrats and Republicans go at each other in Washington. It's a blood bath.

Parents lose all rational thought processes when it comes to their children. I am a parent to two young children, currently 12 and 9, and I know all about mother bear feelings. It has been one of the last terrains I have had to master in terms of trust and surrender. I can be very "Zen" in every area of my life. However, the feelings of protection and defense that arise as a parent have thrown me off balance.

Children inspire so much in us because they give us unconditional love. Many of us have rarely or never experienced unconditional love. When we become parents, we see the promise of what can be. We want to give our children what we didn't have. Some of us learn for the first time what love really is, and that it has nothing to do with what we "get."

As parents, we become extraordinarily invested in how our children develop. This includes how they are treated outside of our home, to ensuring we set up their lives for greater success than what we had. In this process, our emotional identifications can take us out of balance. When I say "emotional identifications," I mean when we allow ourselves to over protect, are overly emotional, and are full of fear something "bad" will happen to our children if we do not intervene. We forget that our children are also divinely loved and protected just as we are. They also chose their life. We don't have to clamp down and fear every interaction they meet with.

On the other side of this topic are people who invest all of their energy to a child essentially to live vicariously through their child. They insist the child do and accomplish things they didn't accomplish. They project their own ideas about what the child should do or become, creating a new karma. The parent is trying to make up for what they feel was lost.

Last week I was at a little league baseball tryout for my 9-year-old son. They aren't really tryouts. It's more about balancing the teams so that all the best players aren't on one team and all the average or lesser players are on another. While the boys were warming up, I watched a lot of the parents throwing balls to their sons, really trying to be encouraging, myself included. I wanted my son to feel confident when his time came to be assessed.

Right next to me was a dad throwing balls to his son, and he was extremely serious. He had his face very close to his son's face, speaking low, intently, and carefully. The boy was clearly getting frustrated with his dad for putting so much pressure on him and requiring him to follow his instructions so intently. Neither one of them was having much fun. I watched that interaction and felt somewhat sad for both of them. Here they were on a Saturday morning with an opportunity to share an experience together and bond more closely together. The dad was making the experience about "achievement" rather than having fun and developing a skill set.

Energetically, this is an example of how people contract frequencies when they are trying to expand frequencies. We get in the way of abundance and the divine infusing possibility into our experience. When we are feeling sad and frustrated, it's all the more difficult to feel powerful and confident. The dad practicing baseball with his son really loves him. He wants his son to do well so he can feel good about himself and be respected by his peers. When he imposes language and behavior that force his son to respond and react in the way he wants him to, he precludes his son from claiming his own abundance. The son has to figure out his own way to garner respect and confidence. His dad was creating the opposite impact.

As parents, we refuse to trust that the same divine consciousness that works in our lives is also working for our children in their lives. That doesn't mean as parents we are not supposed to supervise and guide our children's experience. We still have to play the Energy Game, no matter how much emotion and love we have for our children. We can end up doing far more harm than good by over-parenting or projecting our own fear onto them. One thing is for sure in parenting: our limitations will show up in how we parent. If we have unresolved anger, sadness, or feel like a failure ourselves, we will impose that on to our children.

When we highlight our children's connection to the divine, and teach them how to be in the "flow" of life, it will inspire them to become successful more than our good-intentioned controlling behavior. Sometimes, it's a really good thing when our children don't get what they want, or get the best position on the team, or the lead in the play. These are the lessons that allow our children to learn from their own wisdom and experience. These are the lessons that help children define who they are to themselves. We can't nor should we do that for a child. These lives are their journeys and their opportunities to be the stars in their own lives. We have to provide a space for them to do that.

I have been to many sporting events for my son and daughter. I have watched parents get really worked up over what happens on the field. It's as if they are at the World Series and everything is on the line. I watch divorced parents acting badly in front of children, using them against the other parent. I watch this acting out and realize that many people do not have an idea about balance, and truly acting in a child's best interest. The energies they are consuming and throwing around are toxic. They are creating karma upon karma and delaying the very feelings they really want to experience in their lives.

Before these feelings of protection, people have to make the choice to parent. As with all relationships, in modern times we are dealing with many sets of energies that people did not have to contend with even 100 years ago. Most of us don't even think about the fact that even 60 years ago, we didn't have the birth control pill. We have gone from procreation as a normal and typical way to approach adulthood, including religious programming about it, to a time in history when men and women have real choices about their life.

In additional to gender equality and changes, we are living in a time when the planet is so populated, many experts contend we cannot support the life we have right now. This includes resource distribution, which is something that requires all of our attention. These are considerations that did not exist 200 years ago. In the span of our known history until the last 200 years, conditions have accelerated in such a way on the planet that when people choose to parent, a whole host of considerations begin to come into the equation. Let's begin with the story of Susan.

Susan is a brilliant and sensitive woman who was married to a doctor and worked at an administrative position. She called me after reading a book review in a local newspaper. She had been struggling with infertility for some time. She was scared and looking for answers. In her world, nothing was giving her peace or making her feel better about her "now." She was quite upset and worried about her inability to become pregnant and stay pregnant. She and her husband had already spent enormous amounts of money on IVF (in vitro fertilization) and other costly procedures.

Susan's first question to me was "Am I cursed?" She followed that with "Did I do something in a past life that is causing me to have this experience?" In the three-plus decades I have been doing this work, I have never seen any evidence that such a thing as a "curse" exists. Is there karma to be resolved? Can energy attract to itself? Can conditions create themselves in such a way that we find ourselves having unpleasant experiences? Yes, yes, and yes. These are not curses. Just as with any relationship, if we allow ourselves to be victims, we will be. If an individual has the capacity to take advantage of another if conditions are ripe, they will. Everything I know about how energy works, and how karma develops and resolves, supports the idea that we either consent to or reject energy. If we consent to the idea that curses are real, and that we do not have autonomy over any energy, then we create that reality.

I explained the curse/karma idea to Susan. Then I looked at her past life energy. I saw that she had more than one lifetime where she was quite self-absorbed. When she had children, she didn't do a very good job of taking care of them. She had created a karma for herself that would make it a bit more difficult to get her hands on children again, especially the ones she had lifetimes with before. We do reincarnate with people we know and have been with before. They are not strangers to us. If someone doesn't treat me well, I'm going to think twice before I go hang out with them. Why would I put myself in a situation that is going to be unpleasant? Susan was learning appreciation. Her pregnancy difficulties were causing her to look at her life differently. Even though in real time she was in pain and her self-worth was coming into question, it was an expansive time for her.

As we continued our dialogue, Susan expressed a lot of guilt for spending her husband's money. She also felt responsible for putting them through the emotional exhaustion of trying to become pregnant, or becoming pregnant and being unable to maintain a pregnancy. When she did become pregnant, she would miscarry. They would be back to square one. She was also feeling inadequate as a woman because she could not conceive and carry a child to term. She was becoming embarrassed about it. She was nearly 40 and hearing the thump of her biological clock tick.

When asked about the possibility of adoption or surrogacy, she indicated her husband was not on board with those options. She was locked into pregnancy as her only route to parenting. She was scared.

Susan's husband considered adoption a "less-than" circumstance. If he chose adoption, then he was "less-than too." This idea of becoming a parent through pregnancy is a declaration of a value in life. It is a core cultural belief that many people in Western culture share. Pregnancy is somehow a representation of our virility, our masculinity, or our femininity. When we allow this type of programming to shape our decisions, we limit not only our ability to receive, but we project erroneous concepts on to our unborn child, who will someday be born and carry on those contracted frequencies.

I worked with Susan to help her separate from the programming about her self-worth. We had to talk about the idea that if she didn't have a baby she was less than a woman. We covered a good distance with that. Just giving her permission to have a purpose beyond procreation was empowering. I explained to her that energetically there is no way to fail in this scenario. She will be fulfilled no matter whether she parents or not. "If a woman does not parent, she will not be fulfilled" is one of the fallacies running rampant on the planet.

There are three categories the majority of women fall into energetically. They are these:

1. The woman absolutely must parent. The karmic agreements are so strong, this woman will be a parent. Often this individual has children early in life and has several children.

2. The woman may parent one day, down the road, after other aspirations have been met. This person is an "option" parent. It means they recognize their fulfillment does not have to come through parenting but still may want the experience. Or, they will simply postpone parenting. Often these women have just one child, maybe two.

3. The woman will not parent. These women know early that parenting is not appealing to them. They can be pressured overtly and covertly to consent to parenting, but they ultimately do not.

The good news is that if you are "meant" to parent, and it is important for your spiritual, karmic, and emotional development, you will have a child. It will happen. If it is not important to your spiritual, karmic, and emotional development, it won't happen. Just like all life purpose events, we can't get away from them. They will find us. Women can relax around the procreation idea. If we don't parent, it will be okay. Our lives will still be full. Now more than ever, at this time in history, women can find incredible fulfillment through the contributions they make, just as men have done for thousands upon thousands of years. There are plenty of children on the planet who need care if we want to be that person for a child.

With Susan, I encountered something that I see from time to time, which is, people do not want to be disloyal to the tribe they are in. They would rather participate in a low-level frequency identification then expand into a higher-level identification. They may not be ready, or the implications of expanding are too great, meaning the relationships may not survive. A survival instinct will only allow them to go so far in their expansion. Susan could only go as far as to get some relief, but not all the way to claim a new perspective. She was comparing herself to her female friends who already had children. She was feeling left out and as if she was failing in her life and as a woman. Her answer was to find a way to get pregnant and stay pregnant.

There is a physiological component to all of this. We are hardwired to procreate to sustain the species. We are more than animals. We all have incarnated at this time in history to help elevate consciousness in a very rapid manner. When we consider how rapidly modern life has expanded since the Industrial Revolution, we have a lot of emotional and spiritual catch-up to do to bring balance to the planet.

Susan and I worked together for a period of time, and eventually she did become pregnant and have a baby. She was thrilled and excited to be a mom. After all the struggle, her fears and doubts were quieted. With Susan, as with all people, if we do not want to project our personal karma and challenges on to our children, before we ever choose to parent I encourage all people to consider the following questions:

1. Why do I want to become a parent?

2. What do I think it will give me and do for me?

3. What are my expectations for my child?

4. Do I believe my child has a job to do for me?

5. Am I becoming a parent because I want to, or because I am keeping up with what I am supposed to do?

6. Is parenting my dream or my parents' dream?

7. What does it mean regarding my masculinity or my femininity if I choose not to parent?

8. Do I believe I can put the needs of someone else before me all the time, for 18 years at least?

These questions are important, because underneath many of them lie our beliefs about parenting, our self-worth, and the programming from our culture and our peers. If we do not examine these beliefs, we go into a creative process unconsciously. Most people agree that babies are cute. They see parents playing at a park or having fun with a child and think those moments are all there are, however, it is a long-term commitment that is full of unexpected twists and turns. It is full of feelings we cannot anticipate. Until you become a parent, you cannot know how you will feel.

My client Genevieve came to me several years ago, dealing with very low self-worth. She is a 40-year-old woman, with a young daughter. She is a professional woman, and one of the kindest people I have ever met. She was raised by seven brothers and sisters as her parents were always working to support the big family. Her siblings, being children themselves, were fiercely competitive with one another. They essentially raised her. They raised her with the limitation of children's perspectives.

Throughout her childhood, she was alone a lot of the time. She had to figure out ways to amuse herself and keep herself company. In childhood she developed a weight problem, for which her siblings harassed her unrelentingly. The boys in her family received much more help than she did. Several were put through college, but Genevieve had to earn her own way. That speaks to her determination to succeed in life.

When she first came to me, she had a pattern in her life of allowing people to take advantage of her both professionally and personally. She believed she had to always go above and beyond for people to earn their attention, their respect, or even their love. She would never go against the family code or belief. In one example, she purchased a four-bedroom home for herself and her daughter. Several of her family members felt entitled to move in. Genevieve was unable to say no. None of them contributed financially, and so the financial burden of these family members moving into her property caused her to lose the property.

In the work place, managers and coworkers were constantly requiring that she work excessive hours. It was not unusual for her to work from 7 a.m. to 9 p.m. or later at night. Often her daughter would be in a conference room at her workplace doing homework or playing on an iPad while Genevieve worked. Although she was educated and a trained professional in a position of authority, she often found people calling her judgment into question. The only way she could rescue herself from these positions was to find other jobs. She was unable to stand up for herself, let alone defend herself, or voice her opinion. She felt she had to take whatever was dished out to her. She had absolutely no sense of boundaries.

We began our work together and began talking about what healthy boundaries look like, and what is appropriate and inappropriate in the workplace or in personal relationships. It seemed to have some impact on her professional success. She began to command more authority in her roles. A self-described "fly under the radar" type of person, she began to recognize that speaking up was as much a necessity in her job description as it was to execute her other job tasks.

Throughout the course of our work together, I would often ask Genevieve if she thought about having a relationship. The only relationship she had ever had was with her daughter's father. It ended badly. Her response was "I'd like one, but I'm too fat and don't feel good about trying to find someone. Who would be interested in me? Besides, I have my daughter." She believed she and her daughter would be together forever. She had already pre-determined her daughter's role in her life. Rather than developing the skill to fill herself up, she was requiring and expecting that her daughter would fill her up.

Although Genevieve loved her daughter very much, unconsciously she was using her daughter. All the nights that Genevieve spent at the office until 9 p.m. feeding her daughter take-out and placing her in a conference room alone was setting her up to have the same life she had. She did not learn how to interact socially, how to stand up for herself, or have a voice or defend herself if necessary. Her daughter was spending all her evenings alone in a conference room while her mother worked. Several times when we had appointments, her daughter would come and sit in the waiting area. She was available when Genevieve wanted her to be available, but her daughter's needs were secondary. Genevieve made sure her daughter went to a great school, she was always fed and clothed, and had opportunities placed before her. What was lacking was true connection. Even though she wanted to, Genevieve could barely make room in her life for her daughter.

Granted, being a single mom is one of the most difficult things on the planet. You are the provider of everything, including love, nurturing, playdates, and money. Genevieve had adequate resources. What she didn't have a lot of is self-worth. She allowed others to bully her at the expense of her daughter and their relationship. There were layers of internal dialogue and beliefs that told her things had to be this way.

One day, she came in for her appointment and was very distressed about her relationship with her daughter. She was visibly upset, as she and her daughter had been arguing. It had been going on for a period of time. It was now escalating to a full-on power struggle. Apparently, at one point, out of frustration, Genevieve slapped her daughter. She felt completely out of control and did not know what to do. Her daughter was becoming verbally aggressive with her. She was being defiant and argumentative, and did not want to do her homework or anything else her mother asked. Overall, she was being resistant to her mother. This was terrifying to Genevieve. Suddenly she was faced with a reality that her daughter may not always be there to love and support her in her life.

This is a mistake many parents make: "I'm going to have children and they will take care of me in my old age." We don't know that. We don't have the right to project that on to our children, but many of us do. If we are loving and attentive to our children, the chances are they are going to want to take care of us. We have modeled that to them. If we put them in a room with a bag of food and pay them no attention, that is not a demonstration of connected love. Yes, their need for food and water has been met, but their need for love and connection has not. Genevieve, through her own pattern of self-abandonment, regularly abandoned her daughter, causing her daughter to repeat a version of the experience Genevieve had in childhood.

Often because of Genevieve's schedule, she and her daughter ate a lot of fast food and didn't get time to move their bodies much. Her daughter started developing a weight problem just as Genevieve had. Now, Genevieve's daughter was pushing back on the routine and the life Genevieve had created for them. Genevieve, being smart and a willing spirit, decided it was time to roll up her sleeves and get to work on the business of filling herself up and deepening her approach toward her interaction with her daughter.

I sent Genevieve and her daughter to a therapist. They began to do some deeper work around the patterns in their life. They were able to come to new understandings about how they wanted to progress as a family. Genevieve began a course of work in NLP (neuro-linguistic programming) on her self-worth and claimed a new dedication to learning to love herself unconditionally.

When we become a parent, anything that is not resolved in our life will show up in how we parent our children. Our flaws will reveal themselves. That is the beauty and the catastrophe of parenting. Parenting, like all relationships, are mechanisms for growth. We can use the experience to heal and expand ourselves, or we can contract and refuse to acknowledge our limited belief systems.

Children, as baby beings, choose us as parents. They have agreements with us to grow as well. Often, baby beings have stronger agreements with one parent than another. As with Genevieve, there was a dual agreement between the two of them to help each other heal. Although Genevieve projected a lot of responsibility onto her child, on some level, spiritually her daughter agreed to be in that role. Eventually, she was the catalyst for Genevieve to reach for her self-love with determination. From a different perspective, her daughter was responsible for Genevieve's shift in focus.

This example with Genevieve and her daughter represents the beauty and synchronicity of how consciousness effects love in the human experience. We see hardship and trials as "bad" things. At the end of the cycle, Genevieve is on a path to self-love. Her daughter, who she has known before, consented to come to the planet and help her with this issue. If that is not love, I don't know how else one would define it. When we know we are stepping into the lion's den, and we still choose to do it because it is in the best interest of the individual and the collective, that's about as potent a statement about the power of love in consciousness there is. Love is strong, unrelenting, courageous, and determined. Energetically, when we match the characteristics of love, we become love and we attract love.

Our life reflects a loving existence where love always finds us, rescues us, and brings us to our wholeness and true nature. It's beautiful.

Like all relationships, even with parenting, we can choose to heal and come closer, or we can resist and contract. We make agreements spiritually with our parents and our children before we ever incarnate into this experience. The more we can separate from programming and be guided by our internal navigation, *what "feels" right to us*, we can choose to parent, or anything else, from a place of abundance. Parenting can be one of the richest experiences one can have in the human experience if embraced from an expansive point of view.

When we approach all our relationships from the choice to heal and expand, rather than contract, we complete agreements with family members, rather than continue or create new karma to resolve. We know we have completed an agreement when there is no longer "charge" upon the person or the situation. (The word *charge* means emotional content other than peace.) When we bring all the other frequencies into a benevolent place, a higher vibration, we are complete. We are done. There is no reason to repeat a relationship, a situation, or specific reoccurring dynamic.

If we only consider present time, most all of us can see that when we don't learn a lesson of the heart, we keep creating experiences to cause us to look at the lesson over and again. I have story upon story of clients who have come to me saying, "I keep choosing the same partner over and over." "I keep taking jobs where people don't value me." In the continuum of life, time is not relevant. It's all about whether or not you are able to expand low-level frequencies into high-level frequencies. When that occurs, we are in an expanded state. When we are in an expanded state, contracted vibrations cannot thrive. Once the light is turned on darkness cannot exist.

CHAPTER 11

Healing

"We are healed of a suffering only by experiencing it in full."
—MARCEL PROUST

When most of us hear the word *healing,* we associate it with physical well-being. We think about healing from an illness, a surgery, or some other physical malady. There is a difference between healing energy itself, the process of healing, and useful remedies we consume after we have developed some symptom. Healing is something we choose and we allow. It is our total ability to embrace the frequencies that will encourage us to extricate ourselves from limited patterns in consciousness. I can best describe the feel of healing energy as smooth, insistent, encouraging, and loving. It can also be focused and direct.

As with all tangible experiences, if we are out of balance to the degree that symptoms have developed, it represents an imbalance in our consciousness. Yet imbalances may or may not relate to the symptom. We can't always identify and correlate a physical symptom with an energetic imbalance. We can make good guesses, as there are consistencies in certain patterns. In the healing process, what is most important is that we stay open to healing in terms of what needs to be healed, rather than just the external result of feeling better.

Again, although external remedies and healing modalities can be very useful, those remedies themselves do not heal us. They address the discomfort of our symptomatic experience. We need them. In this awareness lies a contradiction. No one can heal you but you, and, at the same time, no one is more important to us than healers. What healers do is elevate our consciousness. Healing is the removing of lower-level energies in consciousness or the permanent insertion of higher-level frequencies into our consciousness.

There is groundbreaking insight in the realm of healing that was developed by the AIM Program 15 years ago. After decades of research and testing, the founder, Stephen Lewis, discovered a way to identify frequencies that are out of balance in our energy and can result in physical illness. To date, Stephen has identified more than 500,000 frequencies that correlate to illness. To me, two fascinating aspects of balancing frequencies is this:

1. Most of us have frequencies of life-threatening illnesses. It doesn't mean they will come to pass in our physical experience. We also carry forward genetic programming and information from past life experiences. Any of those can be brought into balance.

2. When frequencies of one imbalance are brought into balance, symptoms from a completely different ailment dissipate. What we think might be causing our disease may not be.

I went on the AIM Program about four years ago. I have managed an autoimmune disorder for many years. At one time, it was so unstable that I had to see my doctor once a month for blood tests to monitor my levels.

The very month I went on the AIM program, my condition stabilized. It has been stable ever since. I am on the same dose of medication. I see my doctor twice a year. When I do, it's practically a social visit.

The approach of balancing frequencies deals with the consciousness of the person. Whatever I am in agreement to healing, or that my karma will allow, heals. The AIM program does not heal people or treat people; it brings frequencies into our consciousness so that we can balance those that have been identified as out of balance. For more information on the AIM Program, visit *www.aimprogram.com*.

When I first began this work 30 years ago, I was fascinated with healing and what causes people to heal not just physically, but emotionally and energetically. I have often used myself as a guinea pig to try on different healing modalities. I have experimented with herbs, oils, stones and crystals, hands-on therapies, and psychotherapy. I found all of them to have some value. Some worked better for me than others, and some lasted longer for me than others. I also took on different modalities myself that focus on moving or directing energy so I could experience delivering healing energy in the first person. I began with Reiki, then Aura Cleansing, Chakra Balancing, and finally by channeling healing guides.

During one part of my psychic training, I learned how to connect with my spirit guides, including a healing guide. A healing guide has a slightly different relationship with us than a typical spirit guide relationship. It is much more antiseptic. Spirit guides feel a lot like dear and trusted friends, while healing guides feel more like a doctor you once had that lacked any bedside manner. What follows are my observations based upon decades of experimentation:

1. **Healing is not a one-sided proposition.** I can use a healing modality to move someone's energy around. It can be effective. It is always temporary. If and until the individual assumes responsibility for their healing, it doesn't become permanent.

2. **Healing is a multi-dimensional process.** Our bodies are not in one place, our health in another, our finances in another, and our relationships in another. Our health is a reflection of what we believe and how we treat ourselves. It all originates from our consciousness, which includes genetic components, past lives, ties to our lineage, and karma.

3. **What works for me may not work for you.** I referenced above how I have experimented with many different modalities. I know a lot of practitioners, therapists, and healers of all kinds. Some people have incredible experiences with Reiki, or Shamanic or chiropractic healing. Others find them irrelevant. What is most important is that we are able to stay open to receive what will work for us. This is why our inner guidance is integral to healing. If we only listen to external input about what will work for us, it is hit and miss about whether or not something will help us.

   I have offered my 30 Day Prosperity plan for free to thousands of people. Some people have miraculous results. Some people have minimal results. It all depends upon where each unique individual is resonating in their awareness and where they are on their continuum. Some people need energy work, others need body work, others emotional work, some need coaching, or any combination of these. Our ability to keep an open mind and, even more important, an open heart, is relevant and important to accessing energy frequencies that will cause us to be able to heal ourselves.

4. **Time is not relevant in healing.** When we bring frequencies into balance, no matter what dis-ease exists in our consciousness, it cannot manifest. It doesn't have any charge on it any longer. There are times people can receive treatment for years and never heal from their problem. Other times people can

heal and shift instantaneously. It is when we are ready to take our next step in our karmic process that healing occurs. We consent to it.

5. **Playing the Energy Game makes a difference.** When we insert high-vibration frequencies into our situation, we influence it. If we have a karma to be unwell in this lifetime, perhaps to learn about healing or the value of life, we may have to contend with illness after illness. Yet, we still have the ability to influence outcomes within the structure we have available to us in the lifetime.

   In addition to personal influence, there are a few miraculous people on the planet who seem to have mastered the ability to project healing energy on to others in a profound manner. They are few and far between, and often difficult to access. These high-vibration individuals tend to be in remote areas of the world. There is a reason for this. My experience with high-vibration individuals is that they need a layer of protection from dense and mundane frequencies on the planet. If they lived in high population areas, they would be over-run by the energy of desperate people. They live in areas where those who really want to receive them must go to the effort and expense to seek them out. This significantly limits their exposure to low-level consciousness entities and energies.

6. **Healing is a natural inclination.** We are hardwired to heal. The nature of divine consciousness is love itself. Love is always being showered upon us. Love itself is a healing energy. Even more, we are love. It is in our DNA. The more we can allow love in all forms into our awareness, the more access we have to healing.

   Often we look at healing as an act of achieving something. It is more an act of becoming aware of what is available to us and allowing it to come in. Some of us put up impediments to our own healing by trying to over-control. Or, we are impatient. Impatience and control shuts down our natural intuition about what will work for us. We have to honor our unique process.

7. **The planet has a lot of healers on it right now.** When I use the word *healer,* it doesn't necessarily mean a doctor, or a shaman, or a hands-on healer. I most often use the word *healer* to refer to a person who gives us contributory energy. Or, they have mastered the art of well-being. We all know these people. They are people who make us laugh. They are the first of our friends we call when we have good news or bad news. We know they will celebrate with us when we win, and they will hold our hands when we are hurt. They are people whose personalities are naturally friendly and jovial. They can't help but cheer us up. It isn't even what they say. It's how we feel when we are in their presence.

Then there are healer types who possess an intention to be a force for benevolence. When you are with them, you know you are "held" and given permission to be exactly where you are. These are often therapists, massage therapists, practitioners of the heart, and body workers on all levels.

We all know a person or people in our life that we simply have to invite to our parties. They know how to connect and talk with everyone. They naturally and intentionally give everyone the right to be exactly where they are in their life.

There are many types of healers who do amazing work, in part because they connect naturally or intentionally to different non-tangible entities. I have come across a handful of people throughout my lifetime who live on a frequency I call "angelic." On rare occasion, I have encountered individuals who have angels in their physical system. These people not only vibrate like angels, but they access healing information from a very unique and potent place. They are always in service, often at high levels, perhaps in corporate environments, school settings, or even bureaucratic systems. They have come to the planet to effect change or healing on complex structures. They work deep unconscious levels. Their impact is not always experienced consciously. Suddenly, one day an organization implements a new policy on employee rights or long-standing policies change.

I met a woman on the angelic frequency named Sharon who was working on her PhD. She happened into an expo where I was speaking. After my presentation, she sat down at my booth to have a reading. The first thing I noticed was how high her frequency was. She is likely the most gentle individual I have ever encountered. She radiated a love and tenderness that I can only describe as angelic.

When she spoke, permission, acceptance, and joy emanated from her. It was as if with every word and act she was handling a newborn baby, or carrying a one-of-a-kind fine piece of china that she didn't want to break. She was careful and tender. It felt as she existed in a total state of non-resistance. I knew I was in the presence of someone very special.

I worked with Sharon on and off for several years. She was having difficulty finishing her doctorate. For a time, she thought her delays in finishing her thesis were that she didn't know exactly how to navigate business or where she would want to put herself. She did actually need to understand more about business to be able to deliver her work in the world. Energetically, she already had all she needed to be successful and contributory in life. Through her struggle with business she was creating energy structures that would make it safe for her to go out in the world and express her healing truth and skill. After she worked the energy around this idea for some time, she was able to finish her degree.

When it comes to physical healing, spiritual people can become obsessed with the spirit and forget to attend to the body. Healthy lifestyle choices can go a long way to remaining in good health. Many of us mistreat our bodies and wonder why they fail us. We abandon the needs of our physical self and wonder why our bodies break down. Our ability to tend to our physical self is important. It is a spiritual act to honor the physical. The following common-sense lifestyle choices can make all the difference in our well-being:

1. Moving our body.

2. Food choices that support our well-being.

3. Adequate sleep.

4. Strategies for managing stress and getting it out of our bodies.

5. Honoring our body rather than criticizing our body.

In the area of emotional healing, there are specific things we can do to resolve our internal challenges and move toward healing. The following suggestions do work:

1. **Remember all experiences are equal in consciousness.** The ego says "good, bad, right, wrong." The soul says "all is abundant." When we encounter pain, the divine has presented us an opportunity to expand. Our ability to learn to see the opportunity is how we grow around the pain and expand, that is, become more abundant.

2. **Reach for gratitude.** Give thanks for the opportunity to expand. Feed the powerlessness love and acceptance, either through ritual or some other means of self-support. Acknowledge that what falls away in our life is only making room for something greater for us.

3. **Be kind to yourself.** Don't judge yourself for being wounded or for not knowing everything. Life is a process, not a race. All of us have layers to uncover to heal and expand. That's what we're doing on the planet. We can only do as much as

we can do. That is enough. There is no timeline to meet for anything in your life. The Divine will always deliver what you need. Trust that. Learn to replace worry with trust.

4. **Do not forget where your life comes from (the origin of your wealth).** Regardless of the vehicle (job, spouse, family, and so on), your needs are being met through your relationship with yourself and the Divine. It is quality of this collaboration that determines your abundance.

5. **Acknowledge the one-ness of all things.** There is no us, no them, only the one. Allow the feeling of connection in life to wash over you. You are one wave in the ocean of life. Everything we do affects everything else. See the God consciousness in you. Recognize that as you heal yourself, you heal and expand the whole. You are mighty and powerful just for being you. One person can and does make a difference.

6. **Take time to take care for yourself mentally, emotionally, spiritually, and physically.** This is how you stay awake to connection. It is how you cope with the awareness of your wounds when you see them. It is one big piece in how you recognize your innate wholeness. Finally, ask for insight on how to stay connected to Source.

— CHAPTER 12 —

Surrender

"Surrender to what is. Say 'yes' to life—and see how life suddenly starts working for you rather than against you."

—ECKHART TOLLE

There is a process, an art, and a discipline to mastering surrender. Surrender as we know it implies we have to give something over to someone else, or that we relinquish control or power in some way. Surrender in this context is much more aligned with relinquishing control. That is a great place to begin the dialogue about surrender.

Control is an illusion. We can't control anything. The ego can become skilled at navigating the physical reality in the human experience, but at any given time, in an instant, our lives can be changed by something we cannot control. Edna's story relates this perfectly.

Edna is a wonderful, caring, and dedicated mother. Edna was in her kitchen one year preparing Thanksgiving dinner for her two young adult sons. This was something she did every year. It was a family tradition. She was the matriarch in the family and did a beautiful job preparing a meal the family would enjoy. It was a consistent event that she controlled and managed without a hitch.

One year during the preparation of the meal, the phone rang. Within the time it took her to pick up the phone she went from having two sons to having one son. Her life was forever changed. Thanksgiving would be forever changed. She had absolutely no control over that outcome.

The more we remind ourselves that nothing is promised and that each moment is a gift, the less inclined we will be to control what is. That is really the crux of the matter. All suffering is created by our resistance to what is. When we practice the art of surrender, or no-resistance, we remain in the flow of abundance. When we resist the present moment, we reject abundance.

The ability to surrender isn't necessarily easy to do. We have to take "easy" out of our vocabulary and simply look for what works to help us shift. Surrender takes practice and determination. We are addicted to our emotional body. We default to that reality first and foremost. In the process of surrender or any form of expansion, we have to bring our emotional body into balance, together with our programming and our beliefs. Once we get that balance in place, we can work our way up to and through surrender. As we practice it more and more, we get there more quickly when we need to. How do we know when we need to surrender? What does that look like?

- **We are uncomfortable.** We are mad, scared, frustrated, sad, or angry. Some situation, person, or event has stimulated a potent emotional reaction inside of us.
- **We are looking for someone or something outside of us to make it better for us.** We see this a lot when people have money troubles. "If only so-and-so would give me that thing for free, or give me a loan, or pay for me, I would feel better." These ideas that someone else controls our well-being are band aids to the ultimate question we all have to face: "How do I make myself happy?"

- **Being sick and tired.** Sometimes being sick and tired of our reality is one of the best things that can happen to us. By the time we get there, we are tired. We don't have a lot of energy to struggle left in us. Our only option is to stop resisting and go with the flow.

How do we surrender? What does that look like?

- **Become aware you are resisting.** When we become aware that we are on a loop, that we are worrying and stressing and freaking out, we can stop it.
- **Stop the loop. Get off the hamster wheel.** The following method has worked for me in the past to get off the hamster wheel: From the awareness that I am on a loop, I look at the palm of my hand. Then I take the palm of my hand and gently smack myself in the forehead. Yes, I mean it. I'm not suggesting you have to smack yourself hard in the head. A physical alert is very effective for helping gain our attention and then shift our focus. When I smack myself in the forehead, I get my attention. I make a statement physically and intentionally to myself that I am in a loop and I need to get out of the loop. You can use whatever works for you. It could be a rubber band snapping against your wrist, or doing jumping jacks, or combing your hair. You want to include a small physical activity to mark the moment and gain your intentional attention. The activity just has to be definitive and something you can remember, and do on-goingly. This is a tool to begin to call the loop to an end. In this moment you recognize you are on a loop and you are now going to begin a process to get out of the loop.
- **Have a discussion with yourself and your fears.** There was a time I worried about money relentlessly. I worried about other things too, but money was the big thing. It was stealing my life force and controlling me on many levels. Yet, I was

still consenting to worry as a valid reaction in my life. I began the "smack-of-the-hand-to-the-forehead" to stop my worry loop. Then I began to talk to myself. The discussion I would have looked something like this:

"All right, universe, you want me to miss my rent payment? You want me to lose my car? I know that I cannot be given a learning experience I don't need, so there must be something here I don't see. Perhaps I'll see it later. I am not going to give up my good feelings for one more second. Do your worst. I am not going to that dark place."

I would battle it out inside my head until I finally consented to my *"what is"* reality. Every single time I did this process, within 24 to 48 hours, whatever my concern had been resolved benevolently. The positive outcome trained me and helped me eradicate my addiction to worry.

- **Find your outlet for processing emotion.** Each situation will show up a little differently. If you are invested in a relationship emotionally, or something severe occurs, it can take some practice and creativity to work through your emotional attachment and find surrender. For me, writing is how I process everything in my life. I write a lot of letters (I never send), and I write a lot of articles. When I am having difficulty in a relationship, I always write letters. Again, I don't always send them. As I have a dialogue from my perspective, it helps me understand what I am attached to and what is really coming up for me.

  In the past, I was a professional singer and used music to express myself. I love music because, even though there are lyrics in songs, the music itself, and the process of generating sound with either your body or fingers, causes us to release energy in a wonderful way. We often access the unconscious mind without needing language to decipher what we feel.

The point is that all release does not have to be conscious. There are methods to release that are just as potent that don't involve conscious engagement. I found singing and playing to be a hugely healing experience. I didn't always know what I was healing, but it felt good. That's kind of the whole purpose of healing: to feel better.

When I exercise, it is another great way I process through my feelings. When my heart rate is up, and the endorphins kick in, it's some of my most productive "solving" and feeling-better time. Often, when I start out on an elliptical machine, I'll close my eyes. I really go inside when my body starts moving. That is another way I release.

There is no one way or right way for any person. Mostly, it's helpful for us to have a way to go into our process and release energy. If we can identify what works for us, we can use that to get to surrender. If I'm pent up or upset about something, I will probably write about it. Then, I will go get some form of exercise. Those happen to be things that are good for me in my life. There's no mistake there. I encourage everyone to look at those things that already give them pleasure and likely there is a way to garner an energy release through that activity.

- **Look at what's in it for you and be thankful.** When I suggest to "look at what's in it for you," I mean to be an investigator in your own life. Rather than going to the negative polarity and ask from a disempowered point of view, "Why is this happening to me?" as if you are being punished, turn it over. Ask yourself:

  - What am I feeling?
  - Have I felt this before?
  - When did I feel this in the past?

- How much of this is present time, how much is past-time?
- How old do I feel?

When we slow down enough to look at our situation through this lens, most of us can identify very quickly what the source of our wounding is and why we are being triggered. Once we see the connection in our life, it becomes easier to expand into a different perspective. We recognize it's not just what's happening in the moment that is causing our discomfort.

- **Learn to tolerate discomfort.** Whenever we change, even when it's positive, it can be uncomfortable. Human beings are creatures of habit. Depending upon the study, most experts agree that 90 to 94 percent of all our choices and interactions are unconscious and habitual. I few years ago, I moved from one house to another in the same town. For several months if I didn't really pay attention, I automatically started to drive down the old street to my former house. I'd have to backtrack. This is a simple example of how we create habit and structure to feel safe and secure. When we go out of our comfort zone, even if it's good, we are in uncharted territory. Our brain says to us, "Your survival is in question; resist, this may not be safe." This is part of what makes change so difficult. Without awareness, support, and determination, we are hardwired not to change.

As we point ourselves in the direction of expansion, we have to become skilled with managing discomfort. One of my teachers, Nayaswami Asha, used to tell us a story about her Yogi and how he would go in for dental work without anesthetic. His rationale was that he wanted the discipline and the practice of putting his attention elsewhere. His response was "Life is short, so what if I have a little pain?" That is a very enlightened perspective from someone with an expanded consciousness and skilled in the art of identification with the eternal now. For those of us who are still inching along at the pace most people vibrate at in this lifetime, we have to make room for discomfort at the level we can.

When we feel sadness or resistance to a break-up, a job loss, or the loss of a pregnancy anything that really pulls our heart strings we have to let ourselves experience it, and do what we can to not rush off of the feelings until we understand the totality of the purpose they serve. This takes courage and determination.

- **Be patient and compassionate with yourself.** When we are experiencing emotions on the negative polarity, it's tough. We want to remember that there are no deadlines or benchmarks we are supposed to meet. We are on our own continuum. What matters most is how we feel about ourselves. Yes, we may be in the midst of a crisis, or loss, or large change, but we have to learn to be patient, forgiving, and compassionate with ourselves. Too often, our achievement-based perspectives tell us we should be doing something different or feeling something different than what we are now. Yes, we want to elevate ourselves, but we can't skip over steps in the process. If we embody compassion for ourselves in our process, it helps. It smooths out the path to other elements of the process.

I often tell clients who are punishing themselves to substitute a friend in place of the circumstance or event they are inside of. I ask them if they have the same judgmental perspective with them that they do about themselves. They always say no. Why should there be a double standard?

Last week, I spoke to an elderly client, Vanessa, who told me she was very mad at herself. She started by saying, "Bear with me; I might cry." She went on to tell me that she was supposed to pick up her grown daughter who was renting a car. The car rental agency was right next to a hospital that they both were familiar with. It was five minutes from Vanessa's home. Vanessa left the house and immediately started driving toward a medical facility she often frequented. It was on the other side of town. As she started driving down the road, about 10 minutes in to the trip, she realized she was going to the wrong place. She had to turn around, back track, and make her way to the true destination. Meanwhile, her daughter became quite worried since Vanessa doesn't carry a cell phone. Vanessa did arrive, but 30 minutes late.

Vanessa was so upset that she made that mistake. She thought it reflected that perhaps she was senile or no longer competent. It was a reasonable mistake. Vanessa is a sharp as a tack. As I spoke with her, I had to convince her to not be so hard on herself. I could get about 50 percent of the way with her.

Learning to love ourselves through our missteps and flaws is so important. We are all on the way to somewhere always. The more we can comfort ourselves, love ourselves, and give ourselves to the expansive plight of the soul, the easier time we will have with it all.

Surrender can be something instantaneous, or other times it takes more time. There is no right or wrong about it. The steps I just outlined help. I had a client named Trisha who was very psychic and gifted in this area. She had triplets. They were a surprise. As you can imagine, having triplets is a lot of work. It's beyond exhausting. She was a technical whiz as well, but had to put her career aspirations on hold to parent her babies. Childcare for three kids is an enormous expense. She had a lot of frustration with that. She also had challenges with division of labor with her husband. As she tried to continue her spiritual development, she got to a point at which she was so overwhelmed by life that she decided to back away completely and deny her spiritual truth.

There are all kinds of scenarios and extremes that play out in life. Perhaps Trisha just needed a break, and shutting down was a way to get a break. I think people with dementia and Alzheimer's are also people looking for a break. They just don't want to participate anymore. There isn't a right or wrong to it. We're on a continuum of expansion, always. If we choose to slow down or speed up, so be it. It's what we need, or we wouldn't be allowed to do it. One could say Trisha surrendered to her physical reality. She obviously needed to do that.

In the process of surrender, we have to intentionally welcome it into our life. There is no right pace or rhythm. The natural course of expansion is contraction. Mostly, we have to honor it. If we can accomplish that, it will take us a long way in our process. It is resistance and criticism that are the biggest killers. Those frequencies are so contracted that not much can get in or out when we consume them.

What follows is a brief meditative and affirmative statement you can reflect upon when you find yourself in a contracted space:

I trust that I am supported in all ways at all times in this experience and in my life. Perfect solutions, gentle resolutions, and benevolence flows in and through me, now and always. I receive them with gratitude and appreciation. I open my heart to receive the loving guidance of divine consciousness that is ever present in the universe. I think and act kindly to myself and others. Life is unfolding perfectly for me. I own this awareness completely and forever with love and certainty. So it is.

CHAPTER 13

Joy

"Joy is the infallible sign of the presence of God."
—Pierre Teilhard de Chardin

I asked my 12-year-old daughter what her definition of joy was, and she told me it was being with people she loved, doing things she loved, and having a good time. That sounded pretty good to me too. The constant in her descriptions is "enjoyment of life." There is an appreciation of things that makes us "feel" life is worthwhile and meaningful.

Beyond these sensory experiences, joy is something we can have at any time, no matter what is occurring in our life. Throughout this book, you have read a lot about staying awake to your process. You've read about courage and determination to deal with your wounding. You've read about learning to tolerate discomfort and see the value in it rather than discard it as "bad." You've read about inserting frequencies medicinally in your space, and to take an active role in your healing and expansive processes. You've read that trying to control life is futile. These are the skill sets, the ideals that can bring us to internal joy.

Joy

What is internal joy? It is a state of being that allows us to recognize the divinity and synchronicity of life no matter what is occurring in the external reality. We see value. Unless you are an enlightened being, you are like the rest of us on the planet inching along to a greater state of expanded consciousness. We all have curve balls thrown at us that test our limits. They aren't really tests. They are opportunities for us to expand into greater levels of abundance.

Joy is one of the greatest expressions of appreciation one can have in life. When we become strong enough to hold that perspective, we are joyful. Even when a sad event comes to us to process, our core sense of joy doesn't leave us. We trust the abundance in the universe and we know it exists. That level of trust in our relationship to the divine becomes a self-fulfilling prophecy. Life reflects abundance in everything we see, everything we do, and everything we receive.

In my younger years, I had to heal from a lot of childhood trauma. As I was doing that, in my young adult life, my navigation was a bit off. I was still peeling back a lot of layers of programming. I created a lot of experiences with people who I now consider to be valuable stepping stones in my life. They helped me realize my worth and define myself. At the time, I perceived them as cruel, disloyal, and untrustworthy. I had to grow around those feelings. I had to learn what they all meant in the context of my life. As I kept my attention on healing and learning the principle of 100-percent responsibility for my creations, including my relationships, everything transformed.

I went from having a lot of friends who were not good to me to having friends who were loyal, but perhaps not entirely compatible for me. I continued to search and do my personal work. As I continued on, I have what it is I do now. I have created a world full of love and friendship that surrounds me at all times. My life is a complete reflection of my healed inner viewpoint about myself. I don't want for love and support. It is abundant in my life.

My life is so rich at this point in time, I forget sometimes that people live in realities that don't reflect that type of appreciation and support because I'm not there anymore. I certainly was there a lot in my past. My world reflects my growth. It reflects my healing. Life mirrors my expansion back to me.

I offer this glimpse into my own life because the principles, practices, and ideas that have been shared with you in this book work. You may not have identical struggles or conflicts that I had. You may need to apply the strategies differently than I have. The essence of the message is constant. *The external reality reflects your internal reality. If and until your life feels like you want it to feel, keep looking inside for your answers. Be courageous and determined. It is in your ability to shift how you see things that your external reality will shift.*

The practices offered in the book work. If you give yourself to your expansion, you will discover your own strategies that work even better than the ones I have suggested.

My 9-year-old son had been a thumb-sucker since he was an infant. He had a blanket to comfort him since he was a baby. Given that he was 9, it was really time (for the sake of his dental health) that he stops sucking. For the past year or so, we have been actively trying different approaches to help him. Nothing really worked for him. In spite of that, I used the basic principle of going inside to help him discover his own truth. We often talked about the need to replace one habit with another. We had to find something he could do to soothe himself and to relax that didn't involve sucking. As much as his dentist or I wanted him to stop, *he* had to want to stop. I knew that it had to be his choice. It had to matter enough to him before change would occur. That is exactly what happened. He began thinking about it regularly without my prompting. Often he would bring it up with me to discuss out of nowhere.

A few months ago, he came to me and said "Mom, I realize that most of the time when I suck my thumb it's when I have my blanket with me." I had never noticed that correlation before. Somewhere in our discussions he began to assume responsibility and take charge of his healing process. He began to pay attention to his own cues. He realized the connection.

With that information in hand, we structured a system where the goal would be for him to only have his blanket with him at night time. We would work our way to that end. He began a self-monitoring system for when he watched TV (he always had his blanket at that time). He began to take breaks using his blanket, starting with 10 minutes at a time. Most often 10 minutes would turn to into 20 minutes, and then an hour or more. He began to develop a confidence he didn't have before that he really could do without both the blanket and sucking. We created a rewards chart with different color stickers. It worked very well for him. In a relatively short period of time, he was able to stop his thumb-sucking habit. The key information that caused us to be able to crack the code came from him.

I didn't cave in to the pressure and programming of "experts" who become militant and hyper-concerned about these types of habits. I encouraged my son to find his own answer in his own time. I trusted that he would. When he was empowered to do that, he did.

This story is indicative of how shifts occur for all of us. Now my son has not only stopped the habit, but he feels great about himself. I didn't shame him or punish him into stopping something he already wanted to stop. I empowered him to find his answers. I was patient. He was determined. He did it.

As we learn to embrace joy as a state of being in our lives, it is the little wins we have in life that formulate the foundation and teach each of us how to honor and appreciate our natural rhythms and experience in life. When we don't fight ourselves or allow ourselves to be persuaded by external voices, our voice will always lead us where we need go. That trust, that awareness, brings incredible peace and joy.

Another aspect of living joyfully and that helps us create joy is to acknowledge our connection to each other and the collective consciousness. There is no us, no them—only one consciousness, of which we are a part. We are not the center of the universe. If we talk to enlightened masters about suffering in the world, why it exists, and why we as individuals are going through a divorce or the loss of a loved one, the master will tell us that they cannot be concerned with the suffering of one instance, in one person. They have concern of enlightenment of the entire consciousness. More is going on than our individual experience.

Years ago when I was working on my book *The Heart of Matter: A Journey to Wholeness*, my mentor and editor asked me what my goal was with the book. I replied that I want to improve the lives of my children and my circumstances. She said to me, "Is that all?" At first, I didn't really understand what she meant. She proceeded to talk to me about how prosperity is a shared experience. If I truly wanted to be abundant, I had to focus on the collective, not just getting my needs met. As I meditated and pondered this idea, I recognized how small and selfish my original goal had been. It was a very limited viewpoint about well-being. If I wanted to be abundant, my work and message had to be inclusive to as many people as possible. I had to have the best interest of others, as well as my ultimate goal. Through that broader contribution, my karma and destiny would be benevolent. There is no other way it could be.

Expansion is what we are here to do in life. It takes a lot of energy and can be tiring. Each of us is born with the ever-persistent determination to eradicate suffering. Yet unless something really forces us to ask "Who am I?" or "How is happiness created?" we don't do it. It's not fun to be pushed to the wall to find out what you are made of, but it's a method that works.

The game on the planet is to master the dance of duality. It is a challenge that requires courage. When we talk about the idea of infinity, life after death, and reincarnation, we can hear these ideas, but inherently the mind and body cannot comprehend eternity or the idea of infinity. We can hear these ideas but we only understand them to a certain point. Something else has to take over before we know it on a body level. We have to feel inspired to embrace expanded consciousness.

Enlightened masters say the point of having spiritual leaders like Jesus or Buddha is to inspire us, not to explain to us. It is inspiration that helps moves us into another reality. Charismatic spiritual teachers are meant to touch some part of ourselves that makes us realize what is possible. Therefore, they talk to us about God in terms and conditions we already know.

For instance, we all have deep longings in our heart. We have a deep longing for love, and a longing to be understood and seen and comforted. We want to be appreciated and supported. Enlightened masters will talk about everyday things we do to help us connect to possibility. They will reduce eternal conversations to topics like friendship and romantic love. Romantic love especially will move us into a discussion that allows us to talk about and have interest in enlightenment. All of us can understand waiting for love and having that special love come in. The heart understands that. The thousands of love coaches on the planet are a testament to this. In my business, it is relationships I am asked about most often. The enlightened masters, instead of trying to tell stories to get the definitions right for our mind to grasp, have us connect to the feelings we have of longing or disappointment. These feelings speak a language the heart can understand. They motivate us to continue the expansive journey in the human experience.

We all live in a state of restlessness. Life is not quite what we want. Many of us have conversations with our self, such as "Should I settle for such and such?" "Should I try for something else or someone else?" "This job isn't what it's supposed to be," "This person doesn't quite fulfill it for me," or "I think I'll go over there and try that situation on." We are restless by nature. Wherever we are standing, it's never enough. Wherever you stand, it will never be enough. Until we reach enlightenment, we will not feel complete. It isn't that you can't shift and try to find a situation that's a little nicer. Ultimately, we have to contend with our internal world and examine our expectations and whether we are projecting those onto a situation. When we focus on possibilities, whether it's a new love or a new job, we remain inspired to keep on with our task of expansion in the human experience.

The embodiment of joy is the purest form of connection to consciousness I know. When we allow joy to permeate our perspective, those frequencies bring more to the world than anything else. We unequivocally say, "I trust and honor life. There is a reason and purpose for all experiences. I honor that." Through that awareness, we connect more fully to God. In that connection, we know our purpose, and we feel our impact on the whole. We are at peace. Joy is attainable. We should have it. We can practice getting there through simple tasks such as:

- **Learning to laugh at life.** All of us could take a crash course in not taking life so seriously. Even when it is serious, still being able to find something to laugh about, even if it is ourselves, is meaningful.

- **Practicing spirituality.** Walk the walk and talk the talk. Too often people use spirituality as a buzzword. They read about it in a book or talk about it in a community group, then go out and express in the world as if no book were read and no topic was discussed with any other person. Practice makes perfect.

- **Being generous (when you don't have to).** Giving for the sake of giving is profound. That's the reason. Too often we give to get something. Getting is fun. Giving is the best way to receive. It fills you up from the inside.

- **Seeing life through the eyes of a child (or just remember to be childlike).** Children see the wonder in everything and every moment. When we slow down to marvel at all the miracles life provides, we feel happier. When we notice a beautiful sunrise or sunset, or appreciate the unconditional love of an animal, or look at the beauty in nature, we feel more connected to life, and it reminds us what a miracle life is. That inspires us.

All these types of activities help us practice the feelings we want to embody. The more we go there, the less we will want to be other places. That's the inspiration the heart needs to continue its journey to wholeness through expansion.

With that said, I wish you joy, love, and abundance in all forms. I thank you for the opportunity to share with you. I look forward to your stories and your comments.

With love and appreciation.

INDEX

ABOUT THE AUTHOR

Phyllis King is a Life Management Expert also known as "The Common Sense Psychic." She has mentored tens of thousands of people in 25 different countries. As a speaker and radio host, she is known for her practical and down-to-earth approach. She has been featured on CBS and NBC TV, as well as radio programs across the country. She is the author of four other books, including *Bouncing Back: Thriving in Changing Times* with Dr. Wayne Dyer. Phyllis holds a B.A. in sociology. Her home and private practice are in the San Francisco Bay Area, where she resides with her children.